THE
WEB WIZARD'S
GUIDE TO

MULTIMEDIA

THE WEB WIZARD'S GUIDE TO MULTIMEDIA

JAMES G. LENGEL

Addison
Wesley

Boston San Francisco New York
London Toronto Sydney Tokyo Singapore Madrid
Mexico City Munich Paris Cape Town Hong Kong Montreal

Executive Editor: *Susan Hartman Sullivan*
Associate Managing Editor: *Pat Mahtani*
Executive Marketing Manager: *Michael Hirsch*
Production Supervision: *Diane Freed*
Cover and Interior Designer: *Leslie Haimes*
Composition: *Gillian Hall, The Aardvark Group*
Copyeditor: *Betsy Hardinger*
Cover Design: *Gina Hagen Kolenda*
Proofreader: *Holly McLean-Aldis*
Prepress and Manufacturing: *Caroline Fell*

Access the latest information about Addison-Wesley titles from our World Wide Web site: *http://www.aw.com/cs*

Many of the designations used by manufacturers and sellers to distinguish their products are claimed as trademarks. Where those designations appear in this book, and Addison-Wesley was aware of a trademark claim, the designations have been printed in initial caps or all caps.

The programs and applications presented in this book have been included for their instructional value. They have been tested with care, but are not guaranteed for any particular purpose. The publisher does not offer any warranties or representations, not does it accept any liabilities with respect to the programs or applications.

Library of Congress Cataloging-in-Publication Data
Lengel, James G.
    The Web Wizard's guide to Multimedia / James G. Lengel.
       p. cm.
    Includes index.
    ISBN 0-201-74561-5(pbk.)
    1. Web sites—Design. 2. Multimedia systems I. Title.

    TK5105.888.L453 2002
    005.7'--dc21   2001045799
                                                  CIP

2345678910—QWT—04030201

TABLE OF CONTENTS

PREFACE

About Addison-Wesley's Web Wizard Series

The beauty of the Web is that, with a little effort, anyone can harness its power to create sophisticated Web sites. Addison-Wesley's Web Wizard Series helps students master the Web by presenting a concise introduction to one important Internet topic or technology in each book. The books start from square one and assume no prior experience with the technology being covered. Mastering the Web doesn't come with a wave of a magic wand; but by studying these accessible, highly visual textbooks, readers will be well on their way.

The series is written by instructors who are familiar with the challenges beginners face when learning the material. To this end, the Web Wizard books offer more than a cookbook approach: they emphasize principles and offer clear explanations, giving the reader a strong foundation of knowledge on which to build.

Numerous features highlight important points and aid in learning:

⭐ Tips — important points to keep in mind

⭐ Shortcuts — timesaving ideas

⭐ Warnings — things to watch out for

⭐ Do It Yourself — activities to try now

⭐ Review questions and hands-on exercises

⭐ Online references — Web sites to visit to obtain more information

Supplementary materials for the books, including updates, additional examples, and source code, are available at `http://www.aw.com/webwizard`. Also available for qualified instructors adopting a book from the series are instructor's manuals, sample tests, and solutions. Please contact your Addison-Wesley sales representative for the instructor resources password.

About This Book

The Web Wizard's Guide to Multimedia takes you through the process of planning, preparing, and embedding multimedia into your Web site. It covers images, animation, sound, video, VR and interactivity, along with key overarching issues such as digitization, data compression, and bandwidth. It looks at the different ways that multimedia can be used to communicate ideas on the Web, with many examples to analyze. It then takes you step-by-step as you create the multimedia files, save them in the best format, and include them in a Web page.

For beginners, this book will get you started with multimedia on the Web and introduce you to the basic software programs and techniques. Along the way, you'll learn about how multimedia works on the Web and how your site's viewers might best receive it. You'll see examples of multimedia software, such as Flash, Fireworks, Director, and Shockwave, and learn enough to get started with these programs.

You'll get some instruction in sound and video editing, 3-D and VR scene creation, interactivity, and photo editing. This book won't make you an expert in any one of these techniques, but it will provide a comprehensive overview of how multimedia is created for the Web today.

The techniques and approaches in this book are based on my experience helping thousands of students in three courses at the Boston University College of Communication: Computers in Communication, Designing Interactive Communication, and Multimedia Development lab. To all of these students, I extend my thanks for their hard work and willingness to experiment with the new media. Dean Brent Baker at the College provided needed encouragement and support to these students and me as together we learned what worked best while trying to wrestle the old analog media, such as television, radio, and records, into the new digital networks.

To my colleagues who reviewed the manuscript of this book—Charles E. Hockersmith at the University of Delaware, John Hollenbeck of San Francisco State University, James Q. Jacobs from Central Arizona College, Emily Stern at The College of New Rochelle, Ellen Taricani of Penn State University, and Ray Trygstad at Illinois Institute of Technology—I thank you for your suggestions, corrections, and constructive criticism.

The Web Wizard's Guide to Multimedia is dedicated to Annie, Eileen, Kathi, and Molly who encouraged and supported me in its inspiration and writing.

James G. Lengel
September 2001

CHAPTER ONE

MULTIMEDIA ON THE WEB: KEY ISSUES

The World Wide Web is a multimedia communication system that can transmit images, voice, music, animation, and video as well as text and numbers. In this chapter, you'll learn how the personal computer is transforming itself into a multimedia appliance. Understanding the concepts of digitization, bandwidth, data compression, and file formats is essential to working with multimedia information on the Web. You also need to understand the realities of Internet computers and connections—realities that shape the nature of the multimedia user's experience.

Chapter Objectives

⭐ To understand how a computer connected to the World Wide Web can work as a multimedia communication device

⭐ To learn how digitization applies to multimedia content

To find out how lack of bandwidth affects user perception of a Web site

 To get acquainted with methods of data compression

 To learn about standards and file formats used on the Web

 To understand how users' hardware, software, and attitudes influence their experience of multimedia on the Web

Communication by Multimedia

Multimedia is not new. In a general sense, it's been with us from the start. It's an essential reflection of the human imagination. When we see a picture, we imagine the story behind it. When we read a sentence, we imagine the picture or idea it describes. When we hear music, we feel the emotion it evokes.

The medium is not the message; rather, we create the message in our minds from the raw material provided by the medium. The interest in multimedia on the Web is the latest manifestation of a deep human need to communicate ideas.

The recent invention of personal computers and the networks that connect them provides a new set of tools with which to practice the ancient craft of multimedia communication. You can think of a Web page as a **multimedia** canvas on which you can display not only still images but also animation, video, voice, music, and other sounds—and let your visitors interact with it in a variety of ways.

Indeed, many traditional media organizations use the Web to extend their reach. Newspapers such as *The New York Times* and *Le Monde*, for example, publish a daily online version containing text and images. Viewers can also watch movies on the Web, listen to radio stations such as NPR, and watch television stations such as CNN with full sound and video.

In fact, the Web is the only mass medium that can use all the forms of human communication simultaneously and in combination. A computer connected to the Web can

 Play and record the human voice

 Display high-quality full-color images

 Display text so that it is easily searchable and readable

 Play video

 Perform music

 Engage viewers in interactive operations

No other medium can use all these forms with any quality or consistency. All the other mass media are essentially one-way—broadcast from a centralized source to an audience through a channel that does not permit or enable them to talk back. The Internet, in contrast, is a two-way system, the only mass medium with the ability to be instantly and always interactive (see Figure 1.1). The potential of this combined multimedia appliance is only beginning to be understood and exploited.

Figure 1.1 Multimedia Web Page

This chapter looks at the key technical and social concepts that underpin the Web. The first one, digitization, is the fundamental technical breakthrough that enables the entire enterprise.

⊚⊚ The Role of Digitization

The key technical concept of the Web is **digitization**: the act of converting communication content—an image, an essay, a soccer broadcast, a concerto—into a series of numbers. Digitization makes computers possible, enables the Internet, and opens the doors to the future of communication.

But it wasn't always this way.

Multimedia before Digitization

Before digitization, each form of human communication had its own technology and its own channel. Text was printed and read in the form of newspapers or books. Images were printed and viewed as photographs or illustrations in magazines. Moving images were recorded on film or videotape and viewed in a movie theater or on a television set. Voice was converted to radio waves and received on a radio set.

Each of these technologies and channels evolved separately. Each one developed its own traditions and content and stored and transmitted its content in a specific form that was shared by none of the others. You couldn't, for example, send a television program through a newspaper. In the home, viewers used different devices, often in different rooms, to receive the content. You wouldn't read the newspaper on your television set nor expect to see pictures on the radio. Moreover, each medium was better than others at delivering some forms of content. You wouldn't think of displaying baseball box scores in a movie theater or trying to listen to a song by opening a magazine.

Today, most of us have in our homes at least one radio, telephone, tape player, television, VCR, CD player, and slide projector, not to mention newspapers, books, and photo albums. Most communities have at least one movie house and a theater for presenting live plays and music concerts.

☆ **DO IT YOURSELF   Count Your Media Appliances**

How many media appliances do you have? Go through your home, car, and backpack counting each of them. How many different types of content do they receive? How much of this content is also available on the Web?

Communication is so important to us that we invest thousands of dollars in devices to receive this content—films, tapes, CDs, situation comedies, news programs, stories, and the like. This demand supports numerous industries:

☆ A worldwide film industry, with actors, directors, writers, distributors, and theaters

☆ A television industry at least as vast as that of film and with the added element of journalism

☆ A smaller but lively radio industry, with more than 10,000 stations in the United States alone

☆ A music recording and distribution industry that employs millions, from singers to violinists to engineers to sellers of advertising

☆ A book writing and publishing industry

☆ A newspaper writing and publishing enterprise in almost every community

☆ A live drama and music industry that ranges from community theater to Broadway to rock concerts

These various industries have been built around the unique technologies of each method of communication. For each method, the machinery itself demands a different form of technical application and allows for a different range of creative art. Authoring a film is different from staging a drama, even though both present the same basic forms of communication (gesture and voice). Writing a good news story takes a different mind-set and skill set than authoring a novel, even though both use exactly the same form and technology.

The Importance of Interactivity

When you're consuming mass media, you usually play a passive role. You read, you listen, you watch; you provide no feedback and exercise no control. Seldom can you explore a topic in more depth, change the order of the events, or ask a question of the author.

Ironically, older forms of human communication are more interactive than most modern media. A storyteller can see her listeners' faces as she tells a story. She responds to their expressions by adjusting the pace or content of the story. This **interactive** experience allows the audience some measure of control over the communication. Live drama is another example of a kind of communication that thrives on interactivity. In sixteenth-century London, actors at the Globe Theatre responded to the laughter and sighs and frowns of the audience. It's easy to see that the communication of ideas is richer, more complex, and more effective when it's interactive.

The one-way nature of mass communication technologies and the widening of the audience, however, lessen interactivity. Compared with almost any period in the past, a larger proportion of the ideas communicated today in the United States comes through one-way methods, and viewers have little influence over the experience (see Figure 1.2).

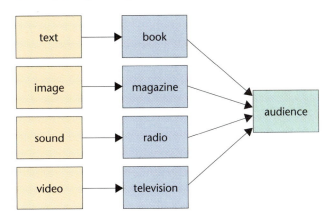

Figure 1.2 Multimedia before the Digital Era

The invention of the personal computer and the World Wide Web offer the possibility of stemming this tide and restoring interactive communication.

The Digital Revolution

In the beginning of the computer age, these new machines had little direct role in the communication of ideas. Only recently have computers and the networks that connect them been widely used for this purpose. The change began with the advent of the personal computer around 1980 and the growth of the World Wide Web in the 1990s.

This most recent communication invention is the most unlike its predecessors. When content is digitized, the characteristics that once distinguished the various media no longer apply. People who communicate using computers and the Web employ a common technology—the digital computer file—to create, edit, store, and transmit their messages. A single medium stores text, voice, video, images, and music, and the computer plays all of them back, with high quality, at the same time (see Figure 1.3). The viewer needs only one device to receive all of the content.

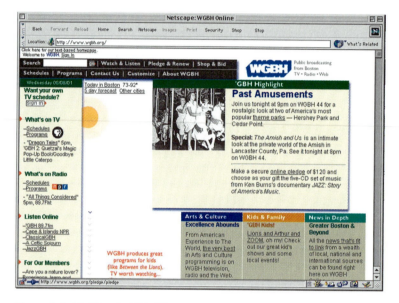

Figure 1.3 Multimedia Web Site

This opens up the possibility of creating new contexts in which communications are received, new forms in which to author it, and new traditions and styles to be developed. It plainly implies the merging of previously separate media.

> ☆ **WARNING** **Access for the Disabled**
>
> Not everyone can see or hear with equal facility. If a multimedia Web site is to serve the widest range of users, including the disabled, it's important that it accommodate those who are visually and hearing impaired. Someone reading your page with a Braille reader, for instance, needs a way to experience the content of images and video. The Web Accessibility Initiative of the World Wide Web Consortium (`http://www.w3.org/WAI/`) provides guidelines on making your site accessible.

How Computers Capture, Store, and Transmit Content

A computer cannot directly record a voice, store an image, or capture a movement. Unlike human eyes or a camera lens, a computer cannot "see." When your eyes or a film camera receives an image, it records and transmits its light in the same form as it arrived. In the photoreceptor cells of your retina or on the molecules on the camera's film, the light creates an **analog** of the image: a copy in the same form as the image itself.

A similar process happens with TV cameras, tape recorders, and radio signals, but each medium uses a unique form of analog and transmits the image in its own way. So you can't put the film from your camera into the TV, you can't play records on your Walkman, and you can't use a radio to read a book.

Computers don't work by making an analogous copy of the original. Instead, they digitize the input that they receive through devices such as a keyboard, microphone, or scanner. They break the signal into tiny pieces and assign a number to each piece. When you scan a photograph, for example, the computer converts the image into a series of **pixels**, or picture elements, with each pixel having a color and a brightness value. Figure 1.4 shows an image on the left and some of its pixels on the right.

Figure 1.4 Pixels in an Image

Here's how it works. Beginning at the upper-right corner and moving across, the computer looks at each pixel, recording its color and brightness as a number. A bright crimson pixel might be recorded as 476, and a dark blue pixel 978. The computer's record of this image is a series of numbers: `476, 476, 476, 474, 473, 471, 460, 320, 320, 670, 978...` and so on. A typical 3 × 5-inch photo would be represented by 80,000 such numbers.

A similar process happens with sound. The computer **samples** the sound every 44 thousandth of a second, recording the pitch and volume of each sampling as a number. The computer's record of the sound is a series of numbers, even more numbers than for a picture. To store 10 seconds of sound requires 440,000 such numbers.

To display the picture, the computer converts the numbers to the appropriately colored pixels. Similarly, to play the sound it converts the numbers to the various pitches and transmits the sound through the speaker.

> **★ TIP**   The word *digitize* is derived from the Latin *digit*, meaning "finger." Just as we count on our fingers, the computer counts via digits. Digitization distinguishes the computer from all previous communication technologies.

After a piece of content has been digitized, the computer saves it and works with it in the same format: as a series of numbers. We've discussed how an image comprises a series of numbers; with text, each letter is represented by a number (A is 65, B is 66, and so forth). Like sound, video is stored as a series of numbers.

After the voice, image, text, music, or video has been converted to digital format, it can be stored on a magnetic disk or CD-ROM. Any part of it can be accessed at random, at any time and any place. It can be sent across networks of wires or satellite relays, and it can be re-created on another computer. It can be copied and edited. The same computer and the same network can handle text as well as sound, and video as well as images. All these capabilities make the computer qualitatively different from previous communication technologies (see Figure 1.5).

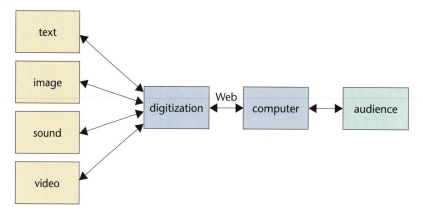

Figure 1.5 Multimedia in the Digital Era

The computer is a single device that can

⭐ Handle all forms of human communication with equal facility

⭐ Combine several forms into a single multimedia work

⭐ Allow interactivity between the viewer and the author

On your computer you can read a novel, hear the news, watch a movie, listen to a concert, or write a letter—all with equal facility.

In short, the computer is the first fully multimedia technology.

◎◎ The Role of Bandwidth

This new technology demands lots of numbers. A quarter-screen video, such as you might find on the CNN or MTV Web site, displays about 80,000 pixels in each frame and runs at about 15 frames per second. That amounts to about 1,200,000 numbers per second (recall that each pixel is represented by a number). And for this kind of digital video, the computer needs 16 bits of information to represent each number. This means that 19,200,000 bits per second must flow through the Internet and onto your computer screen as you watch the video.

Later in this chapter you'll learn about data compression, a technique used by all publishers of Web video to greatly reduce the required data rate. The quarter-screen video just described would typically be compressed to less than 500,000 bits per second.

But even with compression, video on the Web demands considerable **bandwidth**, a measure of how much data can pass through an Internet connection in one second. A typical **modem** connecting your computer to the Internet has a bandwidth of 56 kilobits (often abbreviated 56K) per second. This means that it transmits 56,000 bits of data per second. That's not enough bandwidth to allow real-time viewing of a quarter-screen video with any quality.

The ability of a Web user to experience multimedia depends on the amount of bandwidth available. Low bandwidth, sometimes called a slow connection, prevents many users from watching or listening to multimedia over the Web.

☆**TIP**   Of all the multimedia types, video demands the most bandwidth. Sound is the second most demanding, followed by animations and images. Text requires the fewest bits per second to fill a Web page with information.

Table 1.1 shows six typical Internet connection methods, the nominal bandwidth of each, and the kinds of multimedia it supports. The bandwidths listed here are optimal and not typical.

Table 1.1   Bandwidth and Multimedia with Various Connection Types

Connection	Maximum Bandwidth	Multimedia Supported
56K modem	56 kilobits per second	Images, animation, compressed audio, and very small, highly compressed video
ISDN (Integrated Service Digital Network)	128 kilobits per second	Images, animation, compressed audio, small, and highly compressed video
DSL (digital subscriber line)	512 kilobits per second (at best)	Images, animation, compressed audio, and medium-size, highly compressed video (at best)
Cable modem	512 kilobits per second	Images, animation, compressed audio, and medium-size, highly compressed video
T1 line	1.5 megabits per second	Images, animation, high-quality compressed audio, and large, highly compressed video
Ethernet	10 or 100 megabits per second	Images, animation, high-quality audio, and large compressed video

Most PCs can create and display multimedia full screen and full motion, with high fidelity and high resolution, better than television. Why, then, don't we see sophisticated multimedia on most Web pages? The problem is that high-quality multimedia material often cannot pass through the Internet fast enough for viewing or listening in real time. The bandwidth is the bottleneck.

★ **WARNING** **The Bandwidth Bottleneck**

Although the bandwidth available to typical Web users is growing, it's not yet capable of passing high-quality screen-filling video in real time. But music, voice, animation, and quality images can pass well even through a 56K modem. So Web pages can effectively include multimedia as long as the video is kept within reasonable bounds. For users in offices, schools, and universities, or in homes with cable modems or DSL connections, the full range of multimedia is possible.

At the end of 2000, about half the homes in the United States had Internet access. About 80% were connected with a modem, about 6% by cable modem, 4% by DSL, and 1% by ISDN. The use of the three **broadband** connection methods of cable modem and DSL are growing rapidly. As this book is written, the number of homes with DSL connections is doubling each year. And again, in schools and offices, the proportion of higher-bandwidth connections is greater. The bandwidth bottleneck is abating, and as it does the possibilities for multimedia on the Web are expanding.

A few years from now, as the available bandwidth increases and compression technologies improve, you'll see the gradual easing of these limitations. As you study each type of multimedia in this book, you'll learn about the applicable limitations and the methods of compressing data to use bandwidth wisely.

◎ Data Compression: Why and How

Multimedia on the Web would not be possible without **data compression**. Even the smallest, simplest picture on a Web page is compressed before it is placed on the page and then decompressed by the viewer's computer.

Compression works like this:

1. The author of the Web page digitizes the original multimedia content and saves it as a file.

2. The author compresses the original multimedia file using software designed for this purpose.

3. The author links or embeds the compressed file in the Web page.

4. The user downloads the page, including the compressed multimedia file.

5. The user's browser decompresses the file and transmits it through the computer's monitor or speakers.

6. The user sees or hears the decompressed item.

In most cases, what the viewer sees or hears is not exactly the same as the original content; digitization, compression, and decompression slightly degrade the image, sound, or video. The more a file is compressed, the smaller it gets, the faster it travels over the Web—and the lower its quality. There is a trade-off between compression and quality.

Compression and decompression require the use of **codecs**: software routines designed for this purpose. (The term *codec* comes from the first syllable in *compressor* and *decompressor*.) In most cases, codec routines are included in the programs used by the author and receiver to make and view the file. For example, Photoshop, a popular image editing program, includes a codec that compresses an image file into the Joint Photographic Experts Group (JPEG) format, and the Netscape Navigator browser includes a codec to decompress and display it. QuickTime and Windows Media include several codecs to save video files into various compressed formats, and the browser plug-ins for these programs (discussed later) include codecs to decompress and display the video.

Various codecs are in use, and new codecs are invented every year. The point is that for each codec used to compress the file by the author, a codec must also be available at the other end, on the user's computer, that can decompress the file.

How Codecs Work

Most multimedia compression involves removing data from the file and replacing it at the user's end. Many techniques can be used, but all of them involve one or more of these principles.

Removing Repetition

Most multimedia files involve a lot of repetition. Look at the photograph in Figure 1.6. The sea, the trees on the shore, and the sky contain large areas of the same shades of blue, green, and gray. When digitized, these areas are represented as thousands of pixels of exactly the same color. The string of numbers representing the sky, for example, might include 456, 456, 456, 456, 456, 456 a hundred times over.

A codec looks at this string of identical pixels and reasons, "I don't have to record each one of those 456's. I'll just record '100 456's in a row.' That takes up much less space than a hundred three-digit numbers." In this way, the size of the file is decreased. At the other end, the codec looks at "100 456's in a row" and displays it on the screen as a large area of gray, which to the viewer looks like the sky.

Figure 1.6 An Image with Many Repeated Pixels

Repetition also occurs in music, in animation, and in video; a sustained note in a concerto or an unchanging background in a video can be stored once and followed by the equivalent of "ditto 200 times."

The programming algorithms for compressing by repetition are relatively simple and quick and so are widely used. The Graphics Interchange Format (GIF) codec makes extensive use of repetition, and that explains why the GIF format works best for images containing large areas of solid color.

This kind of repetition is an example of **lossless** compression. When it's done correctly, the pixels in the decompressed file are an exact replica of the original file. No information has been lost or compromised in the process. What the user sees or hears is exactly what the author created. But in complex multimedia compression schemes, repetition is rarely used alone. Instead, it's often combined with some of the other techniques described here.

Averaging

The JPEG format used to compress photographic images makes extensive use of **averaging**. Suppose a photo contains four adjacent pixels that form a square. All four are red, but one is slightly darker than its neighbor, and the third a little lighter, and the fourth the same as the first. Rather than record the four numbers representing the colors of these pixels (for example, 785, 783, 787, 785), the codec averages all four and records 785 × 4, thus saving eight digits and reducing the file size by 67%. Similar averaging can be used in music, voice, and video files.

At the user's end, the codec displays all four pixels in the same color red (785). To the casual observer, the difference between a 785 red pixel and a 787 red pixel is hardly noticeable, so the photo looks close to the original. But it's not exactly the same. Some detail and definition are lost. A careful observer, looking closely at the computer screen, will see a difference between the original file and the one that's been compressed and decompressed with this kind of averaging. This method is called **lossy** compression because some of the original information is gone and cannot be replicated. The trick is to lose information in such a way that the user does not notice that it's missing.

Figure 1.7 Before (Left) and After JPEG Compression

Range Reduction

The first movement of Beethoven's Ninth Symphony starts softly. A few violins play a two-note motif, followed by woodwinds, barely audible, in the back of the concert hall. Then over the next two minutes the volume rises until every instrument is being played as loudly as possible. The sound fills the hall and shakes the rafters. When this symphony is digitized, the volume of the sound is represented by a range of numbers: 1 to represent the softest sound, 255 to represent the loudest. The **dynamic range** of this movement extends across a scale from 0 to 255. Each split second of sound needs an 8-bit number to record its loudness.

But as you digitize the sound, you can create a smaller scale—say, from 0 to 64— to represent the volume so that the movement begins at 1 and peaks at 64. The listener still hears a significant contrast in volume (as Beethoven intended), but the range is not quite as dynamic as in the concert hall. Because you can represent a 64-point scale with a much smaller number than a 256-point scale, you have reduced the amount of data you must save. So you have compressed the file by reducing its range.

⭐ **SHORTCUT**   You can apply range reduction to the relative brightness of the various parts of a photograph or the frames of a video. Unless they have the original to compare it with, most viewers and listeners will not notice the reduction in dynamic range. This technique is used in most audio, video, and image compression codecs.

Selectivity

As you go through life, you notice some things more than others. Your eyes are drawn to objects that move, and you notice the edges of things more than the centers. You perceive certain high-pitched sounds with more alacrity than some lower notes. The wise maker of codecs takes this selective perception into account and saves more information about the things people notice and less information about the things we ignore. By being **selective**, a codec sharply reduces the size of the file with little perception of loss.

Selective compression applies to colors in photos and videos, frequencies in sound, movement in animations, and edges in all forms of multimedia. Combined with the other techniques listed here, it can compress a file while still maintaining adequate integrity.

Frame-Difference Compression

This technique is used mostly in video compression. Figure 1.8 shows a television weathercaster standing in front of a map. The map, which takes up 80% of the frame, never changes; its pixels are identical from frame to frame, second to second, minute to minute. The compression algorithm looks at this consistency and records the weather map's pixels only once, along with an indication of how long the consistency holds.

Figure 1.8 Weather Forecaster

In contrast, the pixels in the meteorologist's arms and face change as he gestures. These changes must be recorded as they occur. In effect, what gets recorded are the **frame differences**: a listing of which pixels change from frame to frame. Because fewer than 20% of the pixels change between frames in this example, there are many opportunities to reduce the size of the file.

Frame-difference compression is often combined with the other techniques to compress video for the Web. Designing these codecs is both a science and an art, with companies such as Sorenson and Qualcomm finding new ways to deliver a multimedia file with adequate fidelity to the original in a greatly reduced size.

Later chapters explain in greater detail how compression works for each of the types of multimedia, and you'll learn how to deploy the various codecs and techniques for maximum effect.

> ☆ **TIP   Codecs**
>
> New codecs are invented every day, so there is no way to understand and master all of them once and for all. These new inventions should be welcomed because they make better-quality multimedia possible.

◎◎ Standards and File Formats

Recall that when a multimedia file is digitized, the data in the file is stored as a series of numbers. Inside the computer, these numbers are converted to **binary** form: a string of 0's and 1's that represent numbers in the base 2 number system. A file in its raw form looks something like this:

```
10010100101001010010100100001010101111101010010100101010010
01001001001001001010010000100101001010101001010101010100101001
0001001010101010101010101010010101...
```

This string of digits would go on and on. A typical Web page image might contain a string of 200,000 0's and 1's—a number that, if printed in this book, would take more than 100 pages. Merely by looking at these digits, you can't tell whether the file is text, a picture, a video, a sound, or animation. They all look the same.

But the beginning of each file is a **header**, which tells the receiving computer what kind of file it is. In effect, the header says, for instance, "This file is a video in the QuickTime format, compressed with the Sorenson codec, and set to display at 320 by 240 pixels." Following the header comes the data representing the pixels and sound samples in each frame of the video. Without the header, the computer wouldn't know what kind of file it was and what format was used for the data.

File Formats

The **format** of a file refers to the way the numbers in the file are arranged. Understanding file formats is a key to making sense of multimedia on the Web.

Multimedia Web files come in a wide variety of formats. Images can be arranged in the GIF, the JPEG, or the Portable Network Graphics (PNG) format (and others). Sound can arrive in the Audio Interchange File (AIF) format, the QuickTime format, or five or six others. Video files can appear in the Windows Media, RealVideo, or QuickTime format, among others.

Dealing with all the different multimedia file formats, and all the codecs used to compress the data, is the bane of Web developers and users. None of the multimedia types enjoys a single, universally agreed-upon file format that works in all browsers and all platforms (discussed shortly). Instead, there are at least three and as many as ten file formats for the various multimedia types, and new ones are being developed.

☆**DO IT YOURSELF**   **Find File Formats**

With your browser, open a Web page that contains multimedia elements, such as the WGBH or Weatherchannel pages pictured earlier in this chapter. Look at the source code, and see how many different file formats you can find. To see the source code, click Page Source or Source under the View menu. Then click Find under the Edit menu to search for `.gif`, `.jpg`, and the other multimedia file formats described in this chapter. How many files of each type did you find?

Any type of file can be sent across the Internet, but Web browsers recognize and display only a few of them. Some formats, such as GIF and JPEG, are recognized and displayed automatically by all the popular Web browsers. Others, especially sound and video files, need **plug-ins**—"helper" programs—to be displayed; by itself, the browser can't handle these files. As new file formats are invented, browsers and plug-ins are updated to accommodate them.

As you study each type of multimedia in this book, you'll learn what the standard file formats are, how they work, and how they're interpreted by browsers and plug-ins.

Multimedia file formats are changing, and new ones are being invented, so you need to stay abreast of developments. It will be a long time before these multiple file formats shake down to a standard set. What's common to all of them is that they carry compressed data that must be decompressed by the user's browser or by a plug-in or other software on the user's computer.

> ☆ **WARNING**   **Use the Right Filenames**
>
> All Web files must adhere to certain naming conventions if they are to be served by servers, transmitted over the Internet, and interpreted by browsers. To be safe, you must choose filenames that will work on all servers and all browsers. The filename must have all lowercase letters and numbers: no spaces, no special characters, and no uppercase letters. And each filename needs a file **extension**, which indicates the file's type: `.jpg` or `.jpeg` for a JPEG image file, `.mov` for a QuickTime movie file, `.htm` or `.html` for an HTML file, and so on.

Standards

All multimedia file formats were invented by an individual or corporation to serve a purpose. At first, they're typically used only by a few people, who go out of their way to install any needed plug-ins. As more people find the format useful, the manufacturers of browsers and system software begin to include the plug-ins in their products.

Some file formats also are adopted by one of the standards organizations, such as ISO (International Standards Organization), IEEE (Institute of Electrical and Electronics Engineers) or the Internet Engineering Task Force (IETF). The adoption of a new file format is voluntary on the part of the software makers and standards organizations; no law or government agency legislates these matters. Usually, it's based on market forces. If hundreds of thousands of Web users have found a new format useful and it has proven to work in a variety of settings, the browser makers and organizations respond to the demands of their customers and turn the new format into a standard.

> ☆ **WARNING**   **Standard? Says Who?**
>
> The inventor or purveyor of a new multimedia file format may claim that it has developed "the new standard in Web video," but until thousands use it and the browser makers and standards organizations support it, such claims are specious.

Some file formats are open standards, whereas others are proprietary. An **open standard** is one whose attributes are made public so that anyone can read and use the format. JPEG and QuickTime are examples. The RealNetworks video format, on the other hand, is **proprietary**: Its attributes are kept secret, and anyone who wants to prepare or stream such video across the Web must pay licensing fees to RealNetworks, Inc. Because both open and proprietary standards are used widely on the Web, this book covers both types.

Web developers can't ignore the realities of standards and market forces in their choice of multimedia file formats. On one hand, you can't present the video on your site in every file format that's been invented. That would take too much work and would be confusing to users. On the other hand, using a single format exclusively would not be wise. Although it would make things easier for you, the single format might not be the best fit for all your users and might not accomplish all of your site's objectives. The best approach is to use the multimedia file formats that best fit the nature of your material and the realities of your visitors' computing environment. To paraphrase an aphorism from the field of architecture, *format follows function*.

Desktop Performance and the User Experience

No matter what file format the multimedia comes in, it's useless if your site's visitors can't experience it. Your Uncle Frank may have invented a cool new file format and compression algorithm for Web video that can play full-screen video at 30 frames per second. But if it works only on Windows 2002 and only in Netscape version 23.5 beta and only with processors of 2 gigahertz and above, then you would be wise not to use it. Because that combination of hardware is rare, few (if any) of your site's visitors would see or hear the video presented in that format. The choice of file formats—indeed, the choice of how and when to use multimedia—must be based on the needs and capabilities of the audience.

The computing resources of Web users vary widely. Mrs. Jones, for example, uses an old laptop with a 640 × 480-pixel screen, connected to the Internet over a telephone line through a 56K modem. Mr. Smith, on the other hand, looks at a 1600 × 1200-pixel display on a computer with a 733 megahertz processor connected to the Web by cable modem. Needless to say, their computing resources are quite different, especially when it comes to working with multimedia Web sites. Mrs. Jones's computer uses an old version of Netscape, with few plug-ins, and if she should encounter an unfamiliar multimedia format she won't reconfigure her computer to receive it. So she avoids sites with lots of multimedia. Mr. Smith seeks out new media, downloads every new plug-in he sees, and is not afraid to install whatever software he needs to view video or animation.

You learned earlier in this chapter about the effect of limited bandwidth. But bandwidth is only one of the issues that affect the reception of multimedia on the Web. Let's look at some of the others.

Display Size

Typically, the smallest monitors show 640 pixels horizontally and 480 pixels vertically; the largest can show 1600 × 1200 pixels. But to get sharper resolution, users with large displays often set their displays to show fewer pixels than capacity. As a result, you have no way of knowing the display size a given viewer is using. Nor is there a way to force the user's computer to the resolution you designed for. So an image or video that fills the screen on one monitor is the size of a postcard on another (see Figure 1.9).

Figure 1.9 A Web Page at 640 × 480 (Left) and at 1152 × 768 Pixels

Processor Speed

It takes quite a few cycles of the computer's processor to decompress each second of sound or video on a Web site. What takes one second to decompress on your computer might take five seconds on your neighbor's. So the clock speed of the processor, and the system software that it uses to access multimedia materials from disk, makes a big difference in the user's experience. In most cases, the faster the processor, the better the experience. But sometimes the opposite is true: For a viewer with an unusually fast processor, your animation might play so fast that it's unreadable.

Video System

After it's decompressed, the multimedia content must be organized into an orderly arrangement of millions of colored pixels or sound samples, which are then sent over the **data bus** (the internal wires that connect one part of the computer to another), placed into random-access memory, and sent to the display. Special video circuitry performs this task, and the nature and speed of this video system vary from computer to computer. So does the refresh rate of the display. All these factors combine to produce subtle but noticeable differences in the ways viewers experience multimedia on a Web site.

User Knowledge

If your site is designed to appeal to typical computer users, the range of their computer knowledge is probably broad. Most people, for example, do not know what a browser media plug-in is. Few people know how to change the resolution of their computer display. Because multimedia often calls for new and unusual software, settings, or techniques, this knowledge gap is widened when users confront sound, video, and animation.

User Willingness

Your visitors may know how to download software or adjust settings but may not be willing to do the work. Seeing your video or hearing your voice may not be worth the time and energy it takes to configure the computer and browser. Variations in user commitment and motivation will result in widely different experiences with your multimedia site.

System Software

Which operating system do your viewers use—Windows 98, Windows 2000, Macintosh OS 9, Windows XP, Windows Me, Unix, or Mac OS X? Each of these systems handles multimedia in its own way. The operating system determines how files are stored and accessed, how windows are opened, how fonts are displayed, and how data is transmitted.

> ⭐**TIP   Which Windows?**
>
> According to *The New York Times*, three-fourths of Windows desktop users had an older version of the system (Windows 98 or Windows 95) in April 2001. Of the remainder, 22% had Windows NT Workstation or Windows 2000 Professional, and only 1% had Windows Me, Microsoft's most recent Windows release at that time. (The numbers came from research firm IDC.)

Browser Type and Settings

Netscape Navigator, Internet Explorer, and the AOL browser interpret Web data differently. A font, image, sound, or video may be displayed in a different size or in a different format, depending on the browser and its preference settings. As you learn about each multimedia format in this book, you'll also explore the specifics of browser displays and settings.

> ⭐**DO IT YOURSELF   Describe Your System**
>
> How is your computer set up for viewing Web pages? Describe your computer in terms of platform, operating system, browser type and version, screen resolution, bandwidth, and processor speed. Are you closer to Mrs. Jones or to Mr. Smith?

Network Configurations and Firewalls

Multimedia on the Web is especially dependent on the way the user's computer is configured on the local area network and on the nature of any existing **firewalls**: network software that is set up to filter Internet data. Some configurations prevent users from downloading or installing multimedia plug-ins, and others restrict browser preferences. Some firewalls, especially in secure corporate networks and schools, do not permit downloading of any sound or video files. These factors contribute to differences in user experience of multimedia.

Plug-Ins

Because plug-in development is a fast-moving field, plug-ins are revised frequently. As a result, many visitors will not have downloaded and installed the latest plug-ins, resulting in a different experience with the Web site.

Computer Platform

Windows, Macintosh, UNIX, Linux; PowerPC, Intel, AMD; Dell, Gateway, IBM, Apple—these are the names of some of the software and hardware that combine to form the **computer platform** on which a user views a Web site. The choice of platform can affect the site's appearance and performance.

In fact, there are so many possible combinations that it's fair to say that no two Web users will have exactly the same experience with your site, especially with its multimedia elements. As this book presents each type of multimedia, you'll learn how you can anticipate and minimize, but not eliminate, these differences in user experience.

⭐ Summary

▶ Multimedia communication, which is just beginning to be implemented on the Web, has a long history. But the capability of interactivity distinguishes the Web from older forms of multimedia communication such as radio, television, film, and photography.

▶ Digitization is the act of converting pictures, sounds, or video into a series of numbers. Digitization enables multimedia on the Web by converting multimedia content into a form that computers can use to store, transmit, and display the information.

▶ Multimedia content demands more bandwidth than does text or numerical data.

▶ Most multimedia content is compressed by the author and later decompressed by the user's computer. Compression methods are a key to good multimedia display on a Web page.

▶ Multimedia content is saved in various standard file formats so that it can be viewed on a wide variety of computer platforms and browsers.

▶ Because of the differences in computers and software, the multimedia experience may differ greatly from viewer to viewer.

⭐ Online References

An explanation of compression and how it works
http://www.howstuffworks.com/file-compression.htm

A technical discussion of MP3, the method used to compress music files
http://www.iis.fhg.de/amm/techinf/layer3/index.html

The latest information and examples of new music and videos on the Web
http://www.launch.com

Examples of film and video on the Web, including many short films in various formats
http://www.ifilm.com
http://www.atomfilms.com

⭐ Review Questions

1. List the similarities and differences in viewing multimedia on the Web as opposed to traditional mass media such as radio, television, and magazines.

2. Explain the importance of digitization in the use of multimedia on the Web.

21

3. Why is the bandwidth bottleneck an important consideration for Web site developers?

4. Why must multimedia content be compressed and decompressed for use on the Web?

5. Explain how a codec works.

6. List at least five file formats used for multimedia on the Web. What kind of data is each used for?

7. Explain how the user's computing setup can affect the nature of the multimedia Web experience.

☆ Hands-On Exercises

1. Visit a multimedia Web site, such as WGBH (`http://www.wgbh.org/`), CNN (`http://www.cnn.com/`), or another site of your own choosing. Make a list of the multimedia elements (images, video, sound, interactivity) that you find on three of the site's pages.

2. Draw a diagram that shows how a photograph is digitized.

3. Visit one of the multimedia Web sites from Exercise 1 at two different bandwidths: first with a high-bandwidth connection such as LAN, DSL, or cable modem, and second with a 28K or 56K dial-up modem connection. Describe the difference in the user experience.

4. Open a high-quality photographic image with Photoshop or another image editing program. Save it in three different compression ratios and formats. Describe the differences in appearance and file size.

CHAPTER TWO

IMAGES ON THE WEB

This chapter explains the important role of images in human communication and outlines a history of the technologies we've invented to create and store images. The bulk of the chapter explains how computer images work and the various methods used to capture and digitize, images for a Web site. The chapter concludes with a discussion of the tools for editing images and incorporating them into Web pages.

Chapter Objectives

- To understand the possibilities for using images in a Web site
- To understand how images are transmitted and displayed on the Web and the roles played by digitization and compression
- To learn the tools and techniques for acquiring and editing images to prepare them for the Web

☆ To find out how to embed, place, and align images in a Web page and create image maps

The Power of Pictures

They were lined up six deep. Grandmothers, teenagers, uncles, and toddlers inched forward to catch a glimpse of the woman behind the bulletproof glass. She wasn't the most beautiful woman they'd seen, and she'd been dead for more than 500 years. It was only her painted image that they'd come to see. They came every day, thousands of them, from Japan, Africa, Canada, Chile. They looked at her and then moved on so that the others could look.

What were they thinking? Why had they come so far? What was it about this image that caused such attention and interest?

The people in the museum were looking at a painting executed by Leonardo da Vinci in the 15th century (see Figure 2.1). But they might also have come to see an Ansel Adams photograph or the Francis Scott Key flag or the stained glass at Chartres. The point is that images compel people's interest in ways that we don't fully understand.

Figure 2.1 Using Images to Explain a Theory about the Mona Lisa

Images come in many different forms.

☆ Photographs capture events, people, situations, moods, or landscapes in ways that our eyes cannot.

☆ Sketches set forth the outlines of motion, shadow, expression, and form, forcing our minds to fill in the details.

☆ Paintings—whether realistic, impressionistic, abstract, monumental, relaxing, somber, or brilliant—use color and light to tickle our eyes and minds.

☆ Symbols represent ideas, social movements, or organizations. The hammer and sickle, the cross, the Stars and Stripes, and the swastika carry immediate connotations.

☆ A corporate logo connects a company's name, products, and image in the mind of the viewer.

☆ A flag is an official image whose colors and patterns carry a special meaning.

☆ A map communicates information on a global as well as local scale.

☆ A diagram is an image that represents a process or a set of relationships in ways that words cannot.

☆ A graph communicates quantitative relationships and brings numbers to life.

People use many types of images every day to communicate ideas, and you should understand the important communicative functions of images before you include them in your Web site. Images can be used to

☆ *Provide facts.* A topographical map, for example, provides an array of facts to hikers that would be difficult or impossible to provide in words. A graph shows revenue growth over time in several categories, giving stockholders important information at a glance. A sketch, a photograph, or a fingerprint can provide the visual evidence that leads to the arrest and conviction of a suspect.

☆ *Explain a process.* The middle-school science site in Figure 2.2 uses a diagram to explain the water cycle. Engineers communicate ideas chiefly through detailed drawings of how a machine works. Flow charts show the path of decision making in a business organization.

☆ *Set a mood.* Winslow Homer's painting *Storm Clouds* creates a mood of loneliness and distance. Pepsi advertisements create the opposite feeling. Rembrandt brings you into the dark interior; Ansel Adams takes you back outside.

☆ *Evoke an idea.* The image of the American flag flying over a besieged fort sparks ideas of war and patriotism. The crucifix reminds the faithful of the powerful concepts of death, redemption, and eternal life. The billowing skirt of Marilyn Monroe crystallizes the innocent optimism of the fifties.

☆ *Pinpoint location.* A map can show you how to get to a house or indicate where France is. A diagram can show you where to sit in my class or where to insert the memory chips into your computer.

☆ *Illustrate relationships.* A flow chart shows who's the boss and who works for whom. A diagram shows how carbon dioxide flows through a leaf in photosynthesis. A pie graph shows how shares are divided.

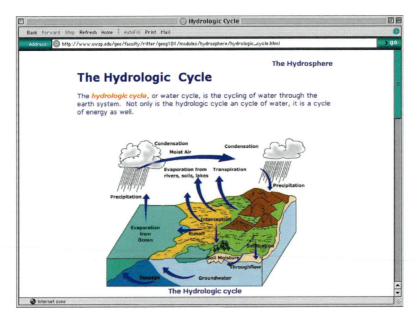

Figure 2.2 Web Page with Image Explaining a Process

★ *Tell stories.* Chips of colored glass tell an illiterate pilgrim the story of a miraculous birth. A photo essay spells out the failure of a government social policy. Four paintings show the passage of the seasons in a garden.

★ *Compare.* Before and after pictures prove the efficacy of the Hair Club for Men. Viewers can see the difference between Van Gogh's strokes and those of Monet. They can see how the Green Mountains are similar to and different from the Cascades.

★ *Identify.* Who's that next to Uncle Harry in the wedding picture? Which one of these faces in the mug book looks most like the robber? Mandy looks so much like her Aunt Susie in that photograph.

Unlike text, images can serve as a universal language that can communicate an idea despite differences in literacy or dialect.

You can incorporate all these functions of images in your Web site to great advantage. But to do so successfully, you need to know how to use a computer to capture all these types of images.

◎◎ Using Images on the Web

Whether images are captured with a scanner, composed in Photoshop, snapped with a digital camera, downloaded through the Internet, or copied from a CD-ROM, the computer stores most of them in the same way: digitally. As mentioned in Chapter One, the image is broken into thousands of pixels. A picture stored this way is called a **bitmap**. (A few images on the Web are stored as vector graphics, using a different format that you will learn about in Chapter Three.)

For its entire life in the computer, a bitmapped image is treated as an array of pixels. When it comes in from the scanner, the camera, or the Internet, it comes into the computer as a string of pixel data. When it is stored on disk, it is stored as a file of numbers, one number for each pixel. When it goes from the disk to the computer's RAM (random access memory), it sits as a series of numbers in thousands of RAM locations. When you edit the image in Photoshop, you're really looking at and changing a huge array of individual pixels. When the image is displayed in the Web page, it's displayed as pixels, about 72 to the inch, each a tiny rectangle on the face of the monitor.

Digitization

Figure 2.3 shows a photograph taken with a digital camera and saved to disk. The entire image is 320 pixels wide and 240 pixels high.

Figure 2.3 Photograph with Close-up of Pixels

The pixels are so small that you can see them in this book only with the aid of a magnifying glass. The close-up in Figure 2.3 magnifies a small area so you can see each individual pixel.

☆ **DO IT YOURSELF   Examine an Image**

Copy an image from your browser to an image-editing program such as Photoshop or Paint Shop Pro. You can do this by right-clicking (Windows) or holding down the mouse (Macintosh) and clicking Copy Image. After pasting it into a window in the image-editing program, zoom in until you can see each pixel clearly.

Numeric Representation

Notice that the leftmost pixel in the top row of the close-up in Figure 2.3 is very light blue with a hint of pink. The computer has assigned this pixel a set of three numbers that indicates its color in terms of how much red, blue, and green it contains. These numbers rank on a scale from 0 to 255. A pure blue pixel would be 0 red, 0 green, and 255 blue. A blue-green pixel would be 0 red, 100 green, and 100 blue.

The pixel in the figure is represented as 133 red, 159 green, and 176 blue. The adjacent pixel is exactly the same color, so it, too, is a 133-159-176. But the third pixel sports a bit more red, less green, and less blue. It gets a 134-155-172.

> ☆ **TIP**   **Hexadecimal Notation**
>
> A computer does not use base 10 numbers to keep track of its colors. Instead, to represent values it uses base 16, which uses the numerals 0-9 followed by the letters A-F. In base 16, the 0-255 color scale is represented over the range 0 to FF. This **hexadecimal notation** (also called **hex**) is used in HTML programming to designate colors. Hex numbers are usually preceded by # to indicate that they are in base 16.

Now look at the dark pixel about seven rows over and ten rows down in the close-up in Figure 2.3. It's very dark, almost black. The computer assigns this one the number 0-3-30. (Pure black would be 0-0-0.) Every pixel in this picture is represented in this way.

On a computer display, each pixel comprises three phosphors: red, green, and blue. If the blue phosphor is lit to its maximum and the red and green ones are dark, you see a bright blue pixel. Lighting the blue and green phosphors and leaving the red dark would result in a blue-green pixel. Lighting all the phosphors to their maximum results in a white pixel. The various combinations allow the display of more than 32,000 colors. Table 2.1 shows how this numbering system works with a few sample colors.

Table 2.1 RGB Numerization

Color	Red phosphor	Green phosphor	Blue phosphor	Hexadecimal	Result
Black	0	0	0	# 00 00 00	
Dark blue	0	0	128	# 00 00 80	
Bright blue	0	0	255	# 00 00 FF	
Blue-green	0	153	153	# 00 99 99	
Medium red	153	0	0	# 99 00 00	
White	255	255	255	# FF FF FFF	

The image shown in Figure 2.3 is stored in the computer pixel-by-pixel as a series of numbers, something like this:

```
#859FB0, #86A0B1, #859FB0, #889BAC, ... #9FB5C3, #3E4F61
...
```

In all, this image contains 76,800 pixels, so in its original uncompressed form it would consist of a string of 76,800 numbers. All this for a simple photo for a Web page! As mentioned in Chapter One, however, most Web images are stored in a compressed format, in which fewer numbers are used. You will learn more about image compression later in this chapter.

To see the numerical values of the pixels of a bitmapped Web image, you can use an image-editing program such as Photoshop. To capture the image, right-click (Windows) or press the mouse on the image (Macintosh) and click Copy Image. Then paste it into the image-editing program and zoom in to see each pixel distinctly. Then use the Info Palette to show the red, green, and blue values of each pixel, as shown in Figure 2.4.

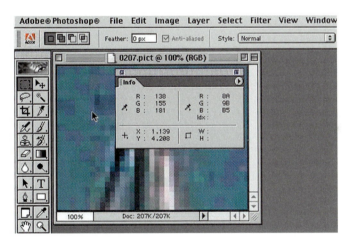

Figure 2.4 Examining Pixel Values with Photoshop Elements

Color Depth

So far we've focused on high-quality, 16-bit color, in which each phosphor of the image is represented by a **16-bit** number such as #9F. With 16-bit color, more than 30,000 different colors can be displayed. (On many computers, this is called "thousands of colors.") Some images, and some older computers, cannot display this many different colors—that is, their **color depth** is not as great—so they represent each value with an **8-bit** number. This shows only 256 colors. The result is a poorer-quality image but one whose file is much smaller and much faster to transmit over the Web. Figure 2.5 shows the same photograph at 16-bit and 8-bit color depth. Can you see the difference in quality?

Figure 2.5 16-bit (Left) and 8-bit Versions of the Same Image

Today's computers can easily display 16-bit color, and advances in compression technology allow Web developers to shrink the file size of such images without reducing quality.

Even greater color depths are available, such as 24-bit and 32-bit color ("millions of colors"), and they give you an even wider range of color. But the increase in image quality at these depths is imperceptible to most viewers of a Web site. So in most cases, photographs for the Web are developed in 16-bit color and saved in the JPEG compressed format.

Other types of nonphotographic images—such as logos, line drawings, and solid shapes that contain little shading or gradients of color—can be prepared at a lower color depth with excellent quality. These are most often saved in GIF, another compression scheme better suited to this type of image. Later in this chapter, as you learn to edit and compress images, you'll also find out how to ensure that your images are at the optimal color depth for your Web site.

☆**DO IT YOURSELF**   **Change Bit Depth**

Use an image-editing program to open an image file from the Web. Reduce its color depth to 8 bits and then to 4 bits by putting the image into the Index color mode and then choosing 256 colors and then 64 colors. Notice the change in picture quality.

Compression Methods

If uncompressed, the photograph in Figure 2.3, with its 76,800 pixels, would send about 250K of data across the Web. For typical modem users, it would take about half a minute for the image to appear. This is too long for most people. As you learned in Chapter One, compression schemes combine several methods to reduce the size of the file as much as possible while reducing the quality of the image as little as possible.

Most images on the Web are compressed with the JPEG or the GIF system. Photographic images are most often compressed as JPEGs, and line drawings are most often compressed with GIF. The PNG format is an emerging compression scheme that works like GIF.

Each method of compression is designed to handle a specific type of image. Even though you can compress a line drawing with JPEG or a photo with GIF, you get the best results if you use the designated method.

How JPEG Compression Works

Because Web developers can't afford to send the full 16 bits of data about each pixel in a photographic image, they must somehow reduce the amount of data imperceptibly. The photographers and computer scientists who formed the Joint Photographic Experts Group designed a set of **algorithms**—mathematical recipes—that are applied to the pixel data to compress the image. The JPEG algorithms follow these steps:

1. Reduce the range of chroma information. The RGB digitization scheme saves 255 levels of chroma (color) information and 255 levels of luma (brightness) information about each pixel. Because the human eye is much less sensitive to color than to brightness, JPEG records fewer levels of color information. The amount of reduction is variable but typically records 64 levels of color.

2. Group pixels into blocks. Most adjacent pixels in a photograph are similar in color and brightness, as you saw in the example of the boat photo in Figure 2.3. Any block of 4 or 16 pixels usually shows little variation. So JPEG determines the average values for the block and saves it as a single number; then, using only a few additional numbers, it records any slight differences from this average for the pixels in the block. So what began as 4 or 16 discrete 16-bit numbers is reduced to 2 or 3 (see Figure 2.6).

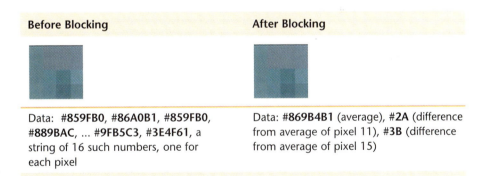

Before Blocking	After Blocking
Data: **#859FB0**, **#86A0B1**, **#859FB0**, **#889BAC**, ... **#9FB5C3**, **#3E4F61**, a string of 16 such numbers, one for each pixel	Data: **#869B4B1** (average), **#2A** (difference from average of pixel 11), **#3B** (difference from average of pixel 15)

Figure 2.6 Averaging Blocks of Pixels

3. Quantize the blocks. After each block has been averaged, the data has been reduced considerably, depending on how large the blocks are and how much difference from the average is tolerated. In most parts of most photographs, adjacent blocks contain similar color and brightness. Rather than repeat the same (or a very close) 16-bit number over and over across the image, JPEG **quantizes** the blocks—that is, it looks at a group of adjacent blocks and cal-

culates the difference of each from the average of all the blocks; in most photos, this is not a very big difference. Then it records those differences using a 4-bit or 8-bit number.

As you save the image in an image-editing program such as Photoshop, you can adjust the level of compression and picture quality, as shown in Figure 2.7. The program manipulates the parameters of the averaging and quantization process. By sliding the triangle to the left, you decrease the size of the file and at the same time reduce the picture quality. Sliding the triangle to the right increases picture quality at the cost of larger file size.

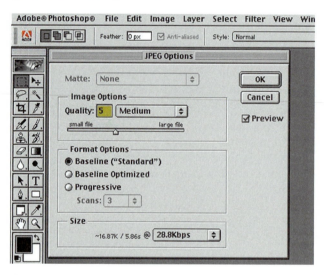

Figure 2.7 Saving a JPEG in Photoshop

A typical photo such as Figure 2.5, saved with a medium amount of compression, would drop from 240K to about 28K—about one-ninth of its original file size. In addition to the parameter settings, the amount of the reduction depends on the nature of the photo. A photo with lots of areas of plain color, such as the one in Figure 2.3, will compress more under JPEG than a photo with more detail and color contrasts, such as Figure 2.5.

The compressed JPEG file is stored on the Web server in its own file, with a Web-legal filename such as `image.jpg`. The `.jpg` file extension identifies the file type, enabling the user's Web browser to decompress it. In most cases, you use HTML or JavaScript code to embed the file in your Web page. Then when the user opens the page, the image file is downloaded automatically.

The JPEG algorithm works in reverse at the receiving end. The user's browser receives the compressed file from the Web server and uses its codec (see Chapter

One) to decompresses and display it pixel-by-pixel on the Web page. First, the codec sets up each block of pixels with its averaged color and brightness; then it goes through each block and re-creates the modifications in each pixel. When this calculation is complete and every pixel has a number, the image is displayed. Decompression takes time, but not as much time as you save by transmitting the much smaller compressed file.

How GIF Compression Works

Compared with JPEG, GIF is a much simpler compression scheme. It starts by reducing the color depth of every pixel to 8 bits or less. This cuts the file size by about two-thirds. The resulting reduction in picture quality is much more noticeable in a photograph (see Figure 2.4) than in a line drawing such as Figure 2.8.

Figure 2.8 Line Drawing Before (Left) and After GIF Compression

Next, the GIF compressor looks for repetition in color across a row of pixels. In Figure 2.8, for instance, all 320 pixels in the top row are exactly the same pure white color. Instead of saving a string of 320 8-bit numbers, GIF saves one 8-bit number to represent the color and then uses only two numbers to save the instruction that repeats that value 319 times. So it has reduced the amount of data needed to represent this top row of pixels from 320 numbers to 3 numbers. That's quite a reduction.

When it reaches the middle of the picture, row 120, it must save more information. The string of numbers for this row includes these instructions: "white, repeated 20 times; red, repeated 50 times; blue, repeated 100 times; white, repeated 15 times; green, repeated 5 times; white, repeated 50 times." That's more data than the top row but far less data than 320 8-bit numbers.

The image on the left in Figure 2.8 is a 16-bit image, at about 240K. Reducing it to 8-bit color cut its file size to 120K. Applying the second part of the GIF compression scheme chopped it further to about 25K.

As with JPEG images, the user's browser receives the compressed GIF file from the Web server and then applies the GIF algorithm in reverse to re-create and then display the image on the Web page. Because fewer calculations are involved, the computer takes less time to decompress a GIF than a JPEG image.

File Formats for Images on the Web

Although JPEG and GIF are not the only file formats that Web browsers can decompress, they are by far the most prevalent. The new PNG format uses algorithms similar to those of JPEG and GIF. The PNG scheme is designed to work best with line drawings, as a substitute for GIF. Compressed with PNG, the image in Figure 2.8 ends up about 20K, a little smaller than with GIF.

Image-editing programs such as Photoshop can compress in any of these three formats. As you'll learn in the next section, the image-editing program takes care of the details of the compression algorithm for you. You need only click Save As or Save for Web from the File menu.

☆**WARNING** **Unrecognized File Formats**

The popular Web browsers can automatically decompress and display images saved in JPEG, GIF, and PNG but not necessarily other image file formats such as TIFF (Tagged Image File Format), BMP (bitmapped), PICT, PCX, PDF (Portable Document Format), or EPS (Encapsulated PostScript). Photoshop can save an image in any of these formats, but only JPEG, GIF, and PNG are handled automatically by browsers. The other formats were designed for other purposes and not for Web pages. You can send them over the Web, but your visitors can't view them if their browsers don't have special software or browser plug-ins.

◎◉ Preparing Images for the Web

No matter what the file format or compression scheme, each image that appears on a Web site must be acquired, edited, and saved. You can acquire images from many sources, ranging from digital cameras to scanned photos to hand drawings. Then you can modify and enhance them using image-editing programs. Finally, you save them in the proper format in the proper place for display in your site.

☆**WARNING** **Whose Image Is It?**

Images, like words, are the property of their creator. U.S. and international copyright laws protect the owner of an image from its use by other people without permission. So when you scan or copy an image from another source, remember that you will need permission to publish it in your Web site.

Image Sources

As a Web developer, you're often called on to use images in a variety of forms from a variety of sources. They might originate as film photographs, drawings, content from other Web sites, pictures taken with a digital camera, clip art and stock photo collections, and still images captured from videotape. Here are instructions for using each of these sources.

Scanner

A scanner digitizes images from photographs, slides, book pages, magazines, paper drawings, even small objects—anything that can be placed on the scanner bed. The scanner shines a beam of light on the item, which is reflected back to a light-sensitive receptor. The scanner divides the image into pixels and records the color and brightness of each pixel as a string of numbers. Then the scanner sends the numbers to the computer, where it is displayed in the scanning software.

To acquire an image from a scanner, follow these steps:

1. Open the scanner software. This might be Photoshop with a scanning plug-in, or a special-purpose program that came with the scanner.

2. Place the item on the bed of the scanner.

3. In the scanner software, set the resolution of the scan. Items that you plan to display on the Web page in their original size should be scanned at 72 dots per

inch (dpi), the resolution of most computer screens. Items that you plan to enlarge should be scanned at a higher resolution—144 dpi if you plan to double the size; 216 dpi if you triple it.

4. Conduct a preview scan. This lets you select only the areas you need to scan.

5. Select the scan area by moving the selection rectangle over the item you wish to scan.

6. Scan the item. You will hear and see the light move across the scanner. A large, high-resolution scan may take a minute or more.

7. Inspect the image in the document window of the scanning software and get ready to edit it.

Most scans will need to be edited, a topic covered in the next section.

Digital Camera

These devices are getting smaller and more accurate, and they can produce photos with more than enough quality and resolution for a Web site. They focus the reflected light from the subject onto an array of light-sensitive cells—one for each pixel—that pick up the color and brightness of the light. The string of numbers produced by this digitization is compressed by software inside the camera and saved on a memory chip or floppy disk. You copy the file from the camera to the computer and open the image in image-editing software such as Photoshop.

The key to the quality of this kind of image lies in the act of taking the picture. A well-composed, well-lit subject will produce a better image regardless of the camera's quality or resolution. Photos for the Web should be closely cropped, clearly lit, and set against a plain background.

The resolution of digital cameras ranges from 640 by 480 pixels to more than 2000 by 1500 pixels. You'll need to edit and resize most images in Photoshop before they're ready for display in your site.

Drawn from Scratch

Original artwork, drawn by an artist, is often used in Web sites. The artist may use a specialized drawing program such as Adobe Illustrator or Macromedia Freehand, or an image-editing program such as Photoshop. She may use brushstrokes or combine and blend images from photos and drawings. No matter how it's created, it must be saved in one of the proper Web formats, such as JPEG or GIF, to be used on a Web site. Because drawing programs often save in EPS and other formats more suited to print, you may have to open the image file in Photoshop, set an appropriate size and resolution, and then save it in a Web format.

⭐ **SHORTCUT**   **Vector Graphics**

Not all images on the Web are saved as in the pixel-by-pixel, bitmapped format. Vector graphics are stored as a collection of lines and shapes that are defined by mathematical formulas. These take up much less file space and can be scaled to different display sizes without loss of resolution. You'll learn about vector graphics in Chapter Three.

Web Sites

You'll find lots of images on the Web, most of them already in proper form.

If you need to use images from the Web, download them with your browser and save them as files on your computer's hard disk without altering their format. You can open these files using your image-editing software, where you can modify and save them in the appropriate format for your site.

Most of the major search engines provide a specialized search for images. At AltaVista, for instance, you click Image Search from the main page. This opens an image-searching tool in which you enter keywords and specify the kind of image you're looking for, as shown in Figure 2.9.

Figure 2.9 Image Search in AltaVista

CD-ROM Collections

Many vendors sell image CD-ROMs (also known as **clip art**), many of them with easy-to-use search engines. The Photodisc Company, for instance, publishes dozens of collections with titles such as "Meetings and Groups," "Vivid Faces," and "Business on the Go." These are high-quality images taken by professional photographers. If you find an image that meets your site's needs, you can view the image for free, and if you decide to publish it on your site you can license it from Photodisc for a nominal fee.

⭐**SHORTCUT**   Most CD image collections supply the images in the proper format and sizes for use on a Web site, so they seldom need editing. Some require no royalty payment beyond the cost of the CD.

Stills from Video

You can extract a still image from a videotape if your computer is equipped with a video-input device. These devices are designed for digital video (for example, a FireWire connection) or for analog video (for example, a video digitizing card). To extract the image, you connect the video camcorder or playback deck to the computer and launch the video-editing software (Adobe Premiere, Apple iMovie, Final Cut Pro, Edit DV, and so on). Play the video, watch it on the screen, and use the software to capture the clip you need. The software allows you to save the clip to the hard disk as an image file.

Depending on the software you use, the formats, sizes, and quality will vary when you use this method. You'll want to open, edit, and save most of these images—using photo-editing software such as Photoshop—before they're ready for use on the Web.

⭐**DO IT YOURSELF**   **Acquire Images**

Acquire images from as many of the different sources listed here as you can. Save them for now. You'll edit some of them in the next section.

Image-Editing Software

No matter what the source, most images will need to be edited before they're ready for use on a Web site. Most Web developers use Adobe Photoshop for this, but other image-editing programs can be used, such as Macromedia Fireworks, Paint Shop Pro, Microsoft Photo, Photoshop LE, or Photoshop Elements. Using these software programs, you can open images from a variety of formats, resize them, modify the colors and elements, combine them with other images, add text and graphics, compress them, and save them in a variety of formats. The more expensive programs have faster and better tools and include special effects, filters, and complex color, text, and shading controls. Table 2.2 shows some of the image-editing programs used by Web developers.

Most of these programs include these tools often used by Web developers:

⭐ **Selection tools** let you select part of an image based on proximity, color, area, or other factors. In Photoshop, these include the marquee to select areas of various shapes; the lasso to outline a user-defined selection of any shape; the magic wand to select areas of similar color; and the Grow, Inverse, Feather, Similar, and Modify items under the Select menu to expand, contract, or change a selection. You use these tools to select part of an image before copying or modifying it.

⭐ **Painting tools** let you add color or pattern to an image. In Photoshop these tools include the paintbrush, airbrush, eraser, pencil, line, text, and paint bucket tools as well as the Fill item under the Edit menu. You select a color or pattern to paint, fill, or write; then you select the appropriate tool and apply it to the image.

Preparing Images for the Web

Table 2.2 A Cross Section of Image-Editing Programs

Program	What the Manufacturer Says	Manufacturer URL
Adobe Photoshop, Photoshop Elements, ImageReady	"Delivering the broadest and most productive toolset available, Photoshop helps you explore your creativity, work at peak efficiency, and achieve the highest quality results across all media."	`http://www.adobe.com/ digitalimag/main.html`
Macromedia Fireworks	"Create, edit, and animate Web graphics using a complete set of bitmap and vector tools. Use export controls to optimize your images, give them advanced interactivity, and export them into Macromedia Dreamweaver and other HTML editors."	`http://www.macromedia.com/ software/fireworks/`
Paint Shop Pro	"Create, edit, draw, paint, animate: Paint Shop Pro offers the easiest, most affordable way to achieve professional results."	`http://www.jasc.com/product. asp?pf_id=001`
GraphicConverter	"GraphicConverter converts pictures to different formats. Also it contains many useful features for picture manipulation."	`http://www.lemkesoft.de/ us_gcabout.html`

★ **Text tools** let you add text in any font, color, size, and style.

★ **Modification tools** let you adjust or change the image. These include the move, smudge, blur, dodge, and burn tools as well as the many items under the Filter, Image→Adjust, and Edit→Transform menus. These tools let you darken, lighten, blend, or revise the image's colors in a variety of ways.

 Resizing tools let you change the size of an image or a selected area. These tools include the Image Size and Canvas Size items under the Image menu, and the Scale item under the Edit→Transform menu.

 Viewing tools let you change the way you look at the image on the screen. These tools include the zoom and hand tools from the palette as well as the items under the View menu.

You can modify most of these tools to use them in different ways. For example, you can adjust the size, opacity, and style of the paintbrush. You can specify a large, soft brush that paints a 20% color wash, a hard, pinpoint brush that paints a solid stroke, and so on. To modify the tools, you use either palettes under the Window menu or select various options as you use the tool. Figure 2.10 shows the paintbrush tool being modified to paint red of 60% opacity with a medium-sized soft brush.

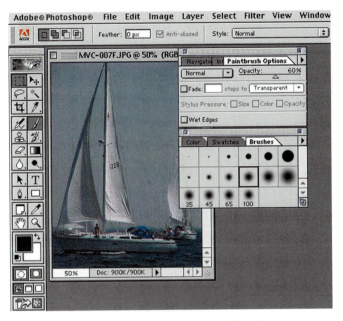

Figure 2.10 Paintbrush Tool and Palettes in Photoshop

☆ DO IT YOURSELF   **Play with the Tools**

Open an image with your favorite image-editing software. Apply each of the basic tools to the image, trying out various techniques and options.

Image-Editing Techniques

Skillful use of the editing tools is the key to producing effective images for a Web page. With most images, you must set the size; adjust brightness, contrast, and color balance; edit for clarity; apply any necessary special effects; and save in the proper compressed format, in that order.

Set the Size and Resolution

Usually, the Web page designer specifies the size of the image using a statement such as "color photo of a sailboat on the sea, 200 by 188." Because the design of the other page elements depends on how much space is set aside for the image, it's important to size it correctly. In Photoshop, click Image Size under the Image menu, and use the dialog box to adjust the image and its resolution.

Most computer displays are set to show 72 pixels per inch, so this is the resolution to use for Web images. Setting a higher resolution will increase download time without improving image quality. You should set the size of the image to the specifications of the design. To achieve the desired size, you may have to crop or modify the image, tasks you can do in Photoshop.

☆**WARNING** Pixelation

If you try to make a tiny picture fill the screen, quality will suffer. A small image an inch square, taken from a Web page, might contain about 5000 pixels. Enlarging this image to three inches square simply fattens the pixels; it doesn't create new detail. The resulting image is **pixelated** (see Figure 2.11), and in most cases not suitable for publishing on a Web site.

Figure 2.11
Enlarged Image
with Pixelation

Edit the Image

After you've set the size and resolution, you need to make sure the image meets the needs of the site and its visitors. Is it bright and clear enough? Are the colors accurate? Does it need some touching up? Now is the time to apply all the image-editing tools and effects described earlier. A good image-editing program like Photoshop can distinguish the sailor from the sea, remove blemishes, and even turn day into night.

But be careful. Too many modifications and special effects can make an image inaccurate or unnatural.

☆**WARNING** The Ethics of Images

Many people think that images, especially photographs, reflect exactly what the camera saw; they think that photographs are an accurate and true depiction of an event. When you start modifying an image, you introduce an ethical question: Is the altered image true and accurate? Darkening the sky, removing people from a scene, or erasing wrinkles makes the image something different from the event it recorded.

Compress the Image

You choose your compression scheme when you save the image, and the image-editing software takes care of the compression details. In Photoshop 6 and later, for instance, you click Save For Web from the File menu to open the dialog box shown in Figure 2.12.

The image shown in Figure 2.12 is being saved in JPEG format, with low quality (10 on a 1–100 scale). The uncompressed image is 900K; the compressed file will be less than 20K. You set each of these parameters to fit the nature of the image and the needs of your audience. Choosing less compression produces a better-looking image, but it will take longer to download. In Figure 2.12, you can see the resulting loss of quality by looking at the edge where the subject's face meets the sky.

Because GIF files use a different method of compression, you must make different choices as you compress and save the file. Figure 2.13 shows the process of saving a GIF image in Photoshop.

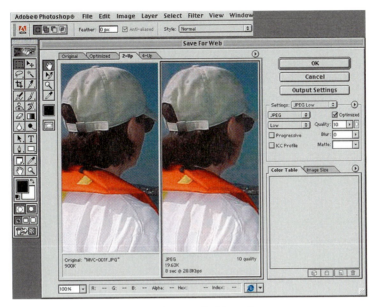

Figure 2.12 Save For Web Dialog Box in Photoshop

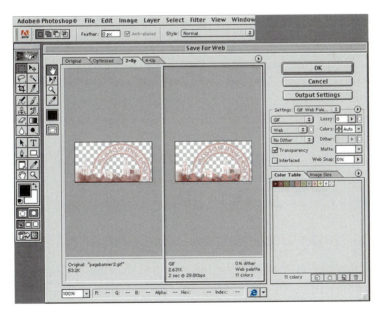

Figure 2.13 Saving a GIF Image with Photoshop

This image is being saved in the GIF format, using a palette of Web colors, with no dithering, in a transparent format. From its original size of more than 50K, compression will reduce this logo to less than 3K, with little loss in quality.

Set the Filename

Filenames are important on the Web, especially for multimedia files. The filenames themselves must be formatted to work properly with all Web servers and browsers, as described in Chapter One. Table 2.3 shows some common filename mistakes.

Table 2.3 Common Filename Mistakes

Filename	Mistakes
Bob's Boat	Lacks a file extension; uses capital letters; uses an apostrophe and a space.
bobsboat.psd	The .psd extension, used for Photoshop files, is not appropriate for images on the Web.
bobsboat.jpeg	The proper filename extension for JPEG files is .jpg.
bobsboat.htm	The .htm or .html file extension is for HTML text files and not for images.
bobsboat/blue.jpg	Uses a slash character.
bobsboat.jpg	This filename looks good.

Save to the Proper Directory

Your images must be saved in the right directory (or folder). Most Web designers set up a directory for multimedia files. For a small site, a single directory named media may be the place for images, sound, video, and other media files. In larger sites, the designer may set up separate directories for images, video, sound, and animations. The image files, in their compressed form, should be saved to the appropriate directory.

⭐ **DO IT YOURSELF**   **Edit Images**

Edit some of the images that you've acquired. Change sizes, add elements, and employ the appropriate image-editing tools. Then save and compress the images in the proper format, with a Web-legal filename, in the appropriate directory.

◎◎ Embedding Images on a Web Page

The images are edited, compressed, and saved in their directory. The next step is to deploy them in the Web site. Images are used in several ways:

⭐ As backgrounds, appearing behind the text and graphics

⭐ As embedded items, often interspersed among text and other media

⭐ As menu items, buttons, or navigation devices such as image maps

⭐ As independent documents that appear in their own browser windows

Each of these uses calls for its own methods for incorporating images. Let's look at using a WYSIWYG Web page editor and HTML to deploy images in each of these ways.

Backgrounds

Figure 2.14 shows a light pink background image of flowers and leaves.

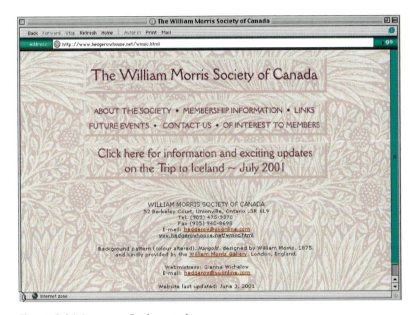

Figure 2.14 Image as Background

This light, low-contrast background image allows easy reading of the superimposed text. The image is essential to the site's purpose; it was created by the artist whose memory this site honors.

To use such an image as a background, you use a WYSIWYG editor such as Dreamweaver. First, you open the Page Properties dialog box and select the image from the directory of images prepared and saved earlier. The image appears, and the rest of the site is built over this background. The HTML code might be

```
<body background="wmsc/images/marigold.jpg">
```

This code specifies that the name of the image file is `marigold.jpg`, it's part of the body of the page, and it's in the `images` directory.

Web Page Content

Figure 2.15 shows photos of eight faculty members for a summer institute. Each of these images, prepared separately, was inserted by the Web developer into a table on the Web page.

☆**TIP**   **Reading HTML**

Most Web pages are written in Hypertext Markup Language (HTML). You can view the HTML code of a Web page by clicking Source or Page Source under the View menu on your browser. The HTML document contains instructions for the browser to follow as it displays the page. The code tells the browser what to put on the page and how it should appear. In the code shown here, `<body>` is an HTML **tag** that tells the browser that what follows is the main part, or body, of the document. `background` is an **attribute** of the body tag; it tells the browser that the body of this page is to display a background and that the image for this background can be found at `wmsc/images/marigold.jpg`, which is most likely a directory on the Web server. *The Web Wizard's Guide to HTML*, by Wendy Lehnert (Addison-Wesley 2001), is a good resource for learning about HTML.

Figure 2.15 Images on a Web Page

To insert such images using a WYSIWYG editor such as Dreamweaver, you place the pointer where you want the image to appear and then click Image from the Insert menu. A dialog box appears that allows you to click the image you want, and you see the image appear on the page. The HTML code would look like this:

```
<IMG SRC="faculty/abramson.jpg" WIDTH=100 HEIGHT=127
BORDER=0 ALIGN=bottom>
```

This code grabs the image file named `abramson.jpg` from the `faculty` directory and places it on the page at 100 pixels wide and 127 pixels high, aligned to the bottom and without a border. `IMG` is the tag, and `SRC` ("source"), `WIDTH`, `HEIGHT`, `BORDER`, and `ALIGN` are all attributes of this tag.

In a Separate Window

An image can appear in its own browser window, such as a map that appears when the user clicks a word in the text of a Web page. This is done by linking the image from the Web page. To accomplish this in a WYSIWYG editor such as Dreamweaver, you select the word you want to link from, click Make Link from the modify menu, and then choose the image file from the dialog box. To make the image open in a new browser window—leaving the original Web page open as well—you set the target of this link to *new* in the Properties window. The HTML code for a linked image, that will open in its own window, would look like this:

```
Directions to the regatta can be found on the<a
href="harbormap.gif" target="new">
map of the harbor</a>.
```

★DO IT YOURSELF   **Place an Image in a Web Page**

Using a WYSIWYG editor or HTML code, create a simple Web page that displays one of the images that you saved earlier.

Alignment and Tables

The images in Figure 2.15 are set in a **table** within the Web page so that they line up neatly in rows and columns. Tables are often used to align images and separate them from other elements on the page. Tables can also serve as templates to ensure consistent placement of items from page to page in a Web site.

It's easy to set up tables using a WYSIWYG editor such as Dreamweaver. You click Table from the Insert menu and then specify the number of rows and columns in a dialog box.

The first four images shown in Figure 2.15 are placed in a four-column table. The HTML looks like this:

```
<TABLE BORDER=1 WIDTH=464>
  <TR><TD><IMG SRC="faculty/abramson.jpg" WIDTH=100
HEIGHT=127 BORDER=0 ALIGN=bottom></TD>
    <TD><IMG SRC="faculty/barrett.jpg" WIDTH=100
HEIGHT=129 BORDER=0 ALIGN=bottom></TD>
    <TD><IMG SRC="faculty/blendon.jpg" WIDTH=100
HEIGHT=120 BORDER=0 ALIGN=bottom></TD>
    <TD><img src="faculty/bobo.jpg" width=100 height=119
border=0></TD>
  </TR>
...
</TABLE>
```

The TR and TD tags set up the rows and columns. The IMG tag places an image, and the SRC attribute identifies the source of the image. WIDTH and HEIGHT attributes determine the display size of the image. BORDER sets the size of the line around the image, and ALIGN tells the browser where to display the image in relation to other items on the page.

☆ **DO IT YOURSELF**   **Align Images in a Table**

Use HTML or a WYSIWYG editor to create a simple Web page with a table of at least three columns and two rows. In this table, display some of the images you created earlier.

Links from Images

Images are often used to **link** your page to other pages on the Web. When visitors click any of the small pictures in Figure 2.15, they're sent to a page that contains a larger photo and a text biography of the faculty member. These small linked images, sometimes called **thumbnails**, work just like hypertext links, and they're created in the same way. In Dreamweaver, you select the image, click Make Link under the Modify menu, and then click the page to link to. Here's the HTML for an image with such a link:

```
<TR> <TD ><A HREF="faculty/abramson.htm">
<IMG SRC="faculty/abramson.jpg" WIDTH=100 HEIGHT=127 BOR-
DER=0 ALIGN=bottom></A></TD>
```

This code links the photo of faculty member Abramson (abramson.jpg) to the Web page abramson.htm, located in the faculty directory. This is the page that displays her biography.

Image Maps

A single image that contains several links is called an **image map**. If you click on Uncle George in the family photo, for example, you're sent to a page that shows his picture and plays an audio file of his singing. Click on the tree in a landscape painting, and you jump to a page that identifies and explains the species. Image maps work by defining certain areas of the image as **hot spots** that link to other pages when they're clicked.

A WYSIWYG editor such as Dreamweaver provides tools for constructing image maps. You select the image, open its Properties window, use one of the map tools to draw hot spots right on the image, and then set the link. Figure 2.16 shows how this works.

☆ **TIP**   Although Figure 2.16 shows a literal map, an image map can be any kind of image.

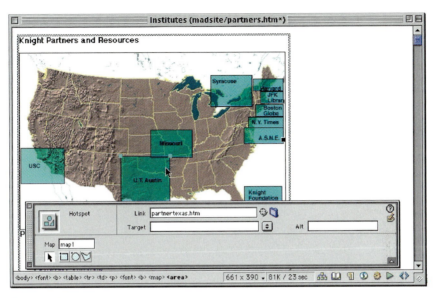

Figure 2.16 Constructing an Image Map with Dreamweaver

Here's the HTML for an image map:

```
<MAP NAME=map1>
<AREA SHAPE=rect COORDS="0,150,73,208"
HREF="partnerusc.htm">
<AREA SHAPE=rect COORDS="165,164,246,262"
HREF="partnertexas.htm">
<AREA SHAPE=rect COORDS="214,122,283,167"
HREF="partnermissouri.htm">
<AREA SHAPE=rect COORDS="301,242,371,268"
HREF="partneruom.htm">
...
</MAP><IMG USEMAP="#map1" SRC="usmaplabeled.jpg">
```

The AREA tag defines the hot spot, with attributes that determine its shape, its coordinates (expressed as x,y values of the upper-left and lower-right corners of the hot spot, relative to the upper-left corner of the image), and its HREF (the file that it links to).

For more information on creating image maps with HTML, see *The Web Wizard's Guide to HTML*.

☆**DO IT YOURSELF**   **Create an Image Map**

Use a WYSIWYG editor or HTML to create an image map from one of the images you saved earlier. Create various hot spots to link to other Web pages and Web resources.

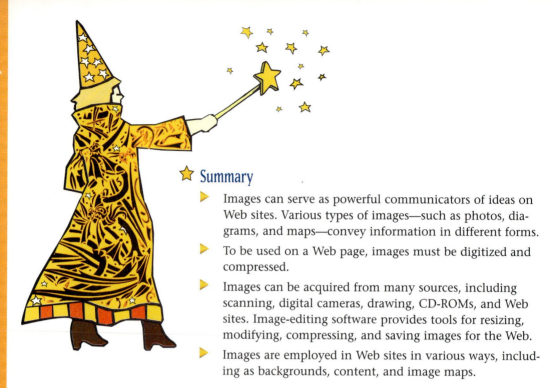

⭐ Summary

▶ Images can serve as powerful communicators of ideas on Web sites. Various types of images—such as photos, diagrams, and maps—convey information in different forms.

▶ To be used on a Web page, images must be digitized and compressed.

▶ Images can be acquired from many sources, including scanning, digital cameras, drawing, CD-ROMs, and Web sites. Image-editing software provides tools for resizing, modifying, compressing, and saving images for the Web.

▶ Images are employed in Web sites in various ways, including as backgrounds, content, and image maps.

⭐ Online References

Frequently asked questions about the JPEG compression scheme
http://www.faqs.org/faqs/jpeg-faq/part1/

Frequently asked questions about image compression
http://www.faqs.org/faqs/compression-faq/part2/

ZDNet Graphics Software Guide
http://www.zdnet.com/products/filter/guide/
0,7267,1500133,00.html

CNET Image Editing Software Reviews
http://www.cnet.com/software/1,11066,0-429627-12020,00.html?
tag=st.sw.429606.dir.429627

About Guide to Graphics Software
http://graphicssoft.about.com/cs/imageediting/

⭐ Review Questions

1. List at least five functions that an image can perform on a Web site.

2. Explain what a pixel is and how it applies to preparing and displaying images on the Web.

3. When would you use GIF compression, and when JPEG? Why?

4. How does the GIF compression algorithm work differently from that of JPEG?

5. List at least three sources for acquiring images for a Web site, and explain why each might be used.

6. Explain how to use at least three tools in a typical image-editing program such as Photoshop.

7. Outline the dangers of pixelation.

8. Explain the process of embedding an image in a Web page, either with a WYSIWYG editor or with HTML.

☆ Hands-On Exercises

1. Find Web sites that use images for each of these functions:
   (a) To explain a process
   (b) To set a mood
   (c) To compare and contrast
   (d) To provide facts and information
   (e) To tell a story

2. Acquire an image from at least three of the following sources: digital camera, scanner, Web site, CD-ROM, video clip, and drawing from scratch.

3. Open the image you acquired in Exercise 2 in an image-editing program that lets you zoom in. Identify the numerical representation of some of the individual pixels.

4. Save an image in three different forms: very high quality, medium quality, and low quality. Describe the method you used to achieve each level of quality, and specify the file size of each version. Then describe the differences you see between the versions.

5. Embed at least five different types of images in a Web page, giving them proper filenames. Create a table to align the images. If possible, create an image map to link parts of an image to other Web resources.

CHAPTER THREE

ANIMATION ON THE WEB

This chapter explores the various kinds of animations used in Web sites, explaining how they work and how they're created. The chapter looks at the leading animation authoring systems and describes how to program Web animations and include them in Web pages.

Chapter Objectives

- To understand the different forms of animation that are used in Web sites
- To find out how animations work
- To learn how to create simple animations with the leading animation software tools
- To be able to embed animations in Web pages

Possibilities and Examples of Animation on the Web

From animated banner ads to complex diagrams of scientific processes, animations are all over the Web. They serve many purposes, from flash and sizzle to serious education. For the purposes of this chapter, **animation** refers to anything that moves on the screen except video (covered in Chapter Five) and interactive games (covered in Chapter Six). An animation can be as simple as a word that flashes on and off to a full-screen graphical experience with musical accompaniment.

Animations can be divided into three types:

★ Those designed to capture the viewer's attention, entertain, or promote

★ Those designed to explain a system or process

★ Those designed to set a mood or create an on-screen environment

Animations That Entertain and Promote

Ever since someone discovered that people pay more attention to on-screen graphics that blink and move than to static images, Web designers have used animation to capture attention and entertain viewers. A typical example is the "shoot the monkey"—type banner ads that pepper the pages of many commercial sites, as shown in Figure 3.1.

Figure 3.1 Shoot the Monkey-Type Banner Ad

The monkey (or the snake or the automobile) scampers across the banner, and text encourages the viewer to click the monkey to win a prize. In most cases, the click results in a **click-through** (link) to a commercial site where the sponsor has placed advertising. The movement of the object captures viewers' attention, and the seeming test of skill and the prize offer entice them to click. This kind of animation can appear anywhere on the page and need not be an essential part of the design because it's not an integral element of the site.

Figure 3.2 shows a small animation of a person setting up a videoconferencing system on a desk. It's found on the Web site of a vendor of such systems and is designed to entertain interested visitors and promote the service.

In addition to capturing attention, this animation helps convey the site's purpose.

Entertainment can take many forms: a little thrill, a little laughter, a surprise, a familiar face, or a happy dance. A simple animation like this can turn a static Web page into a pleasant experience. But these kinds of animations also have a dark side: Displayed repeatedly in a never-ending loop, they can distract the viewer from more important elements of the page. If they're very large, they can also consume valuable bandwidth.

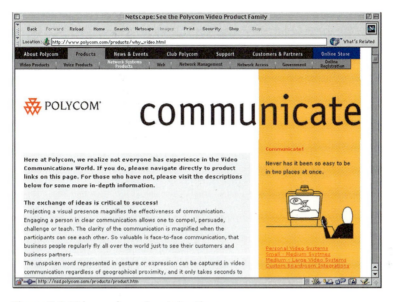

Figure 3.2 Videoconferencing Animation

Animations That Explain

Do you know what goes on inside a leaf when it manufactures sugar from sunlight and water? If you need a refresher on the intricacies of photosynthesis, you can go to the Biology Place (`http://www.biology.com`), where interspersed among the words is an animated diagram that shows the inputs and outputs (see Figure 3.3).

Here, the purpose is not to entertain but to explain. The technologies used to create and display the animation are similar, but the purpose is very different. This diagram took more effort and more screen space, so you'll find fewer animations of this type than the smaller, simpler animations. Other animations might show how to change the oil in your lawn mower or make a long splice in a three-strand rope.

Explanatory animations can be dynamic and complex, approaching the experience of viewing television. Figure 3.4 shows a snapshot of animation from the Cinemetrix Web site (`http://www.cinemetrix.com/target.html`). This animation not only fills the screen but also features voice and music and lasts for several minutes. It explains the company's products.

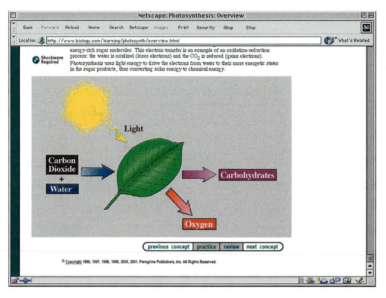

Figure 3.3 Photosynthesis Animation

Figure 3.4 Scene from Cinemetrix Animation

Possibilities and Examples of Animation on the Web

★ **DO IT YOURSELF**   **Find Explanatory Animations**

Find on the Web two or three animations designed to explain a process or guide you through a series of steps. How does each one help accomplish the site's purpose?

Animation That Sets a Mood

People who visit the Web site of the band Phish (`http://www.phish.com/`) encounter a full-screen experience with moving visual elements, sound, images, and text, all of it animated and coordinated to capture the mood of the group's music and lifestyle. It's entertaining, and it explains the background and purpose of the group—but its real purpose is to set a mood. Although we can't make the images move in this book, a snapshot of the animation is shown in Figure 3.5.

Figure 3.5 Mood-setting Animation at the Phish Site

Similar animations—most of them using vector graphics (explained in this chapter)—appear on the sites of many corporations and organizations. In this case, the animation is not essential to the Web page; it *is* the Web page. Difficult to produce and demanding of bandwidth, such animations are not used without careful planning and major investment of time and screen space. They often require a special plug-in (see Chapter One) and a long download time. But they can provide a Web-viewing experience more like film or television and far different from the static text and images found on most Web pages.

☆ **TIP   Plug-ins**

Complex animations, video, sound, and interactive games usually require plug-ins such as RealPlayer, QuickTime, and Shockwave-Flash. Most plug-ins can be downloaded for free from their authors.

☆ **DO IT YOURSELF   Find Mood-Setting Animations**

Explore the Web until you find a screen-filling animation designed set a mood. How does it help accomplish the site's purpose? How long does it take to download? Does it require a special plug-in?

In this chapter, you'll learn how these three kinds of animations work, how they're created, and how they're incorporated into a Web page.

◎◎ How Animation Works on the Web

Two kinds of animation technologies are used on the Web: frame animation and vector animation. The two types are created with different tools, compressed in different ways, and saved in different file formats.

Frame Animation

The simplest form of Web animation, **frame animation** displays a series of still images, or **frames**, one after another in rapid succession, giving the impression of motion. Figure 3.6 shows five of the frames that make up the part of animation shown in Figure 3.2.

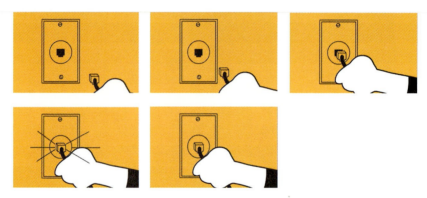

Figure 3.6 Still Images from a Frame Animation

Notice that each frame is only slightly different from the preceding one and that some parts of the image are identical across the entire series. The artist who created an animation like this drew six separate pictures, each defined pixel-by-pixel as a bitmapped image; then the artist combined and saved them into an **animated GIF** file. This special type of GIF image contains the information from all six frames, along with timing information, in a compressed format. Web browsers interpret this file and play back each frame in the proper time sequence.

The size of a frame animation file depends on the size of the image, the number of frames, and the extent of change from frame to frame. The more frames, the larger the image, and the more motion, the larger the file. So this method doesn't work well for large animations that last a long time because the file size would be too large for easy downloading.

Most banner ads and other small, attention-seeking animations are created in this frame-by-frame manner and saved in GIF format. The next section shows you how to use simple software tools such as Photoshop, GIFAnimator, Animation Shop, or GIFBuilder to create your own animation.

☆**DO IT YOURSELF**   **Analyze a Frame Animation**

Find a simple GIF frame animation on the Web. Download it to your disk (right-click on Windows, click and hold on Macintosh, and then click the desired animation from the drop-down menu). Then open this GIF file with GIFBuilder, Fireworks, or GIFAnimator. Inspect each frame to see how the artist created the impression of motion by varying the image from frame to frame.

Vector Animation

Vector animation, the more complex type, is used when objects move across a defined path, or **vector**, on the screen. The artist first draws the object and then defines its path. The object is defined mathematically (for example, *a 40 × 60 rectangle of color #09 FF 66*), as are the path (*a parabolic curve starting at 12,34 and ending at 56,45*) and the speed (*120 pixels per second*). In this way, a few numbers can define a lengthy and complex animation that would consume hundreds of separate frames. No bitmap is created, nor is a series of frames to be played back one at a time.

Viewers play a vector animation using a plug-in. The most common plug-in of this type is Macromedia Flash, which takes the mathematical definition of the object, draws it, and then moves it across the screen in accord with the path definition. Figure 3.7 shows a vector animation being created with Fireworks. You can see the object and the path.

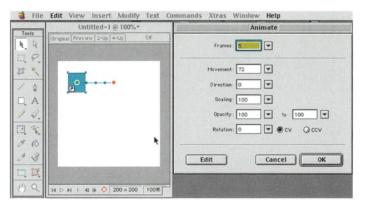

Figure 3.7 Object and Path in a Vector Animation

A vector animation can be much larger, contain more moving objects, and last longer than a frame animation of the same file size. The screen-filling animations that create a mood on a Web site are usually vector animations. Vector animation works best when regular, solid-color objects move in smooth paths. These animations can be saved in very small files; all that's needed are the few numbers that define the object and the path. They download very quickly and display efficiently and quickly in a browser.

Compression Methods

Vector animations contain only the few numbers that define the object and its path, and so they have little need of compression. But frame animations need compression just as images do. An uncompressed file for a simple 100 by 100-pixel animation consisting of 20 frames would comprise 200K, much too large for efficient downloading. Such animations are usually compressed with the GIF algorithm, as described in Chapter One. First, each frame is compressed in the same manner as a still image. Then frame-difference compression is applied.

The combination of the GIF and the frame-difference compression schemes results in animations that load and display quickly. This technique works best with simple line drawings and solid colors. Using it to compress animations made from photographs or complex drawings with lots of movement yields poor results. These kinds of images may often compress better with a video codec such as Sorenson Video, which is designed to compress a series of natural moving images. It uses techniques that you will learn about in Chapter Five.

☆ **SHORTCUT**   The software that creates a vector animation performs the compression automatically as you save the file. You need not worry about vector math or frame differences or the GIF algorithm; they're applied by your animation program. Often, you can adjust the amount of compression, as described in Chapter Two.

☆ **DO IT YOURSELF**   Analyze Animation

Download a simple GIF animation from a Web site. (Many banner ads are GIF animations.) To download, right-click (Windows) or hold down the mouse (Macintosh) on the animation, and then click Download or Save from the menu. Open the file with Photoshop 6, GIFBuilder, or GIFAnimator, all of which can display the individual frames. Analyze the nature and extent of the changes from frame to frame.

File Formats for Animation

The choice of file format for an animation is based on the software program that was used to create it. Animated GIFs are saved in the GIF format with the `.gif` extension and can be displayed without any special plug-ins. The screen-filling, mood-setting animations are most often saved in the Flash format with the `.swf` extension and require the Flash Player plug-in. Animations can also be saved in the PNG format—Fireworks uses PNG as its native mode—but not all browsers support all aspects of this format, so its use is not widespread.

Animations can also be saved in a video format such as QuickTime (`.mov`) or RealVideo (`.ram`), both of which require plug-ins but can also synchronize the animation with sound. You may also find complex, interactive animations saved in the Shockwave format (`.dcr`) if they were created with Director.

You save animations in a directory that's part of the Web site and then embed them in your Web page using a WYSIWYG editor or HTML code. This process is covered later in this chapter.

◎◎ Preparing Animations for the Web

Many software programs can be used to create animations, and new ones are being invented. In this chapter, you'll look at five tools that represent the range of available approaches. You'll build a simple frame animation with Photoshop and then with GIFBuilder (similar to GIFAnimator). Then you'll build a simple vector animation with Fireworks and a more complex one with Flash. You'll learn how to use QuickTime to turn a series of still images into an animation, and how to use a 3-D program such as Cinema 4D to create a 3-D animation.

Building an Animation with Photoshop

Photoshop Elements can be used to create and save simple frame animations. Each frame of the animation is prepared as a **layer** in a single Photoshop document. The layers are then organized automatically by Photoshop (version 6 and later) into an animated GIF and are saved in a format suitable for inclusion in a Web page. Follow these steps:

1. Create a new Photoshop document sized to fit the animation, at a resolution of 72 pixels per inch.

2. Draw or paste the first frame of the animation.

3. Create a new layer from the Layer menu.

4. Draw or paste the second frame. Often, the second frame is quite similar to the first. In this case, you can copy the first layer, go to the second layer, paste, and then modify the second layer so that it is slightly different from the first.

5. Create a third layer, and draw or paste the third frame of animation (see Figure 3.8).

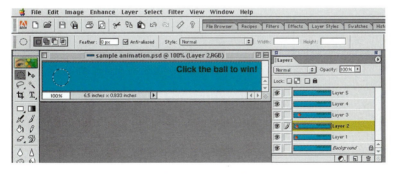

Figure 3.8 Building an Animation with Photoshop Layers

6. Repeat steps 3, 4, and 5 for each frame.

7. When the layers are complete, click Save for Web from the File menu.

8. Click GIF as the file format, and click the Animate box.

9. Use the arrows to leaf through the frames of your animation.

10. Set the frame delay to adjust the speed of the animation.

11. For an animation that never stops, click the Loop box.

12. To see your animation in action, click Preview in Box to open the animation in a browser.

13. Return to the document window to edit your animation as necessary.

14. When you're satisfied with your animation, click Save for Web from the File menu.

15. Give your animation a Web-legal filename with the `.gif` extension, and save it into the proper Web folder.

Photoshop's layer-by-layer approach allows you to see one layer at a time or to view them all at once, something that's helpful in getting each frame to be just a little different from the one before it. As Photoshop saves the animation, it optimizes and compresses it automatically so that its file size is reduced and it downloads quickly.

A GIF animation created in this way with Photoshop will play in both Netscape and Explorer with no plug-ins necessary. Later in this chapter, you'll learn how to include this animation in a Web page.

Building an Animation with GIFBuilder

With GIFBuilder for the Macintosh, like GIFAnimator on Windows, you can't create images, but you can assemble a series of existing images into an animation and then compress and save it in the proper form. The process works like this:

1. Obtain or create a series of images that will form the frames of your animation. These can come from any source: the Web, Photoshop, clip art, even a digital camera.

2. Edit the images so that they are all the same (preferably smaller) size, at a resolution of 72 pixels per inch.

3. Import the images one by one by clicking Add Frame from the File menu. (Alternatively, you can copy each image and then paste it into the GIFBuilder window.)

4. Click Start from the Animate menu to see the animation in action.

5. Use the Options menu to set looping, transitions, and other effects.

6. In the Frames window, click on the interframe delay numbers to adjust the speed of the animation (see Figure 3.9).

7. Edit the animation as necessary, animate it in the Preview window, and revise it until it works correctly.

8. Click Save from the File menu to save the image in animated GIF format.

GIFBuilder offers no drawing tools, but the ability to preview the animation and to adjust its effects and parameters makes it a valuable addition to your toolkit.

Figure 3.9 Creating an Animation with GIFBuilder

Building an Animation with Fireworks

Fireworks' strength is in creating vector animations that produce lots of movement at a small file size. This program includes both drawing tools and control tools and can save animations in a variety of file formats for the Web. Here's how to build a simple animation with Fireworks:

1. Create a new Fireworks document of the appropriate pixel size, at a resolution of 72 pixels per inch.

2. Use the drawing tools to create an object in the document, or paste an image copied from another source. Figure 3.10 shows the palette of Fireworks drawing tools.

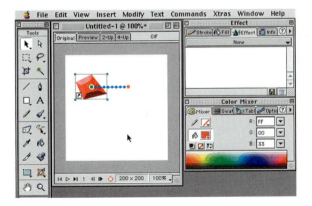

Figure 3.10 Tools and Windows in Fireworks

3. Modify the object using the transformations and effects under the Modify menu and in the Effects window.

4. Animate the object by selecting it and then clicking Animate from the Modify menu.

5. In the Animate dialog box, specify the nature of the animation by typing the number of frames, movement, direction, scaling, and rotation.

6. Preview the animation by clicking the white arrow at the bottom of the document window (see Figure 3.10).

7. Create additional objects and animate them as described in steps 1 through 6.

8. Edit the animation to fit your needs.

9. Save the file in the PNG format.

10. Usually, you will also export the animation, saving another copy in one of the more common Web formats. To save as an animated GIF, click Export Preview from the File menu. Then set the type of file to export, use the arrow to preview it, set the parameters to fit your needs, and save the file to the appropriate Web folder.

11. To save in the Shockwave-Flash format, click Export from the File menu, and then click Macromedia Flash SWF from the Save As pull-down menu.

Building an Animation with Flash

Flash includes not only tools for drawing and transforming objects but also a complete set of animation and control tools. It also supports interaction; you'll learn about that in Chapter Six.

Here, you'll learn how to construct a simple vector animation using this versatile program. The example is small and simple, but the tools and techniques employed here can also be used to create screen-filling animations. Flash includes a complex set of tools and techniques; you'll see only a few of them in use as you build this animation.

Flash works with a set of windows in which you build and control the animation. You place and view the animation objects in the **stage**. The **timeline** shows the frames of the animation you've built; in this timeline, time moves from left to right. Frame 1 happens first, followed by frame 2, and so forth. The timeline window also includes **layers**; each layer contains an object in the animation. Other windows provide tools for working in these two main windows: The **tool palette** provides drawing tools, the **controller** lets you move the animation frame by frame, and the various **inspector** windows let you change the attributes of objects that you create.

Follow these steps:

1. Create a new Flash document.

2. Click a drawing tool from the tool palette.

3. Draw an object on the stage. A new layer appears in the timeline window. This is the layer for the object you just created. Note that the object appears in frame 1. The place where you drew the object is the beginning point of its animation.

4. To animate the object, create additional frames for it to move in. Click layer 1, frame 10 in the timeline, to select it.

5. Click Keyframe from the Insert menu. This creates a keyframe at layer 1, frame 10, and extends the object across to frame 10.

6. Use the arrow tool to select frame 10. Then click and drag the object to the ending point of the animation (see Figure 3.11).

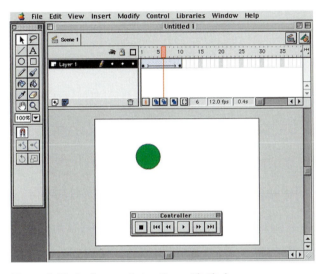

Figure 3.11 Ending an Animation with Flash

7. Shift-click to select frames 1 through 10 of layer 1.

8. Click Create Motion Tween from the Insert menu. This creates all the intervening frames between 1 and 10, placing the object at the proper spot on each frame so that it looks as if it's moving.

9. Use the controller window to rewind the animation to frame 1, and then click the forward arrow to watch the animation play. You should see the ball move across the screen from its beginning to its end point.

You can save this simple animation in several ways. Saving it in the native Flash format, with the file extension `.fla`, makes it useful only to Flash and a few other programs. But this format is important because it saves all your editing so that you can reopen the animation for further work and editing.

When the animation is complete and ready for inclusion in a Web page, it should be saved in a file format that can be displayed by Web browsers. Flash can export animations in many different ways, including those shown in Table 3.1.

Table 3.1 File Formats for Flash Export

File Format	File Extension	Relative Size	Comment
Flash movie	`.swf`	Smallest	Most efficient, but requires browser plug-in
QuickTime movie	`.mov`	Largest	Imports into many programs, requires browser plug-in
Animated GIF	`.gif`	Medium	Requires no plug-in

No matter which format you use, the file should be saved in the proper Web site directory.

So far, you've seen a simple animation. Flash's strength, however, lies in creating complex animations. For instance, each object that you create with Flash can be transformed in a variety of ways. You can add a gradient fill to a shape. You can rotate a shape as it animates, or make it grow bigger over time. You can add many layers, with many different objects that all animate at once. You can define a custom path for the object to follow.

For example, to make the object you animated move along an irregular path, follow these steps:

1. Open the Flash (`.fla`) file you created earlier.

2. Select the layer that contains the animated objects.

3. Put the **playhead**—the red line that shows where you are in the timeline—in frame 1.

4. Click Motion Guide from the Insert menu. This creates a new layer into which you will draw a path that will guide the object.

5. Use the pencil or brush tool to draw a curved line in this layer. Start the line in the exact center of the object (see Figure 3.12). The line will not show in the finished animation.

6. Use the arrows in the controller window to preview the animation as the object moves along the line.

7. Save the animation.

Flash can also be extended to add sound and interactivity, topics covered in Chapters Four and Six.

Creating an Animation with QuickTime Pro

To quickly create an animation from a series of still images, you can use the QuickTime Player application that comes as part of the low-cost QuickTime Pro download. These images can come from any source: the Web, a digital camera, a photo CD, clip art, Photoshop files, and other image-creation programs. Follow these steps:

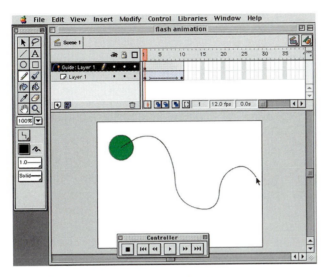

Figure 3.12 Animating along a Path in Flash

1. Make sure all the images are the same size, and put them all in the same folder.
2. Rename the image files in numerical order, such as image1, image2, image3, and so on.
3. Click Open Image Sequence from QuickTime Player's File menu.
4. Click the first image in the series, as shown in Figure 3.13.
5. Click the speed of the animation in frames per second (or seconds per frame).
6. Preview the animation by clicking the Play button.
7. To change the size or other attributes of the animation, click Get Info from the Movie menu, and then use the two pop-up menus to make adjustments.
8. When the animation is complete, save it in the QuickTime (.mov) format. It can be read by all browsers but requires the QuickTime plug-in.

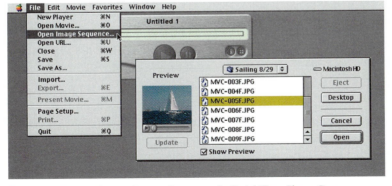

Figure 3.13 Creating an Image Sequence in QuickTime Player Pro

Creating a 3-D Animation

The animations you've created so far are two-dimensional—they move in a single flat plane. You can also create three-dimensional Web animations in which objects appear to move in three dimensions. For the example, you'll use Cinema 4D, a simple and inexpensive program.

As shown in Figure 3.14, Cinema 4D provides a variety of tools and windows to create the objects to be animated and then to move them in space. The objects are shown on x, y, and z axes in the View window.

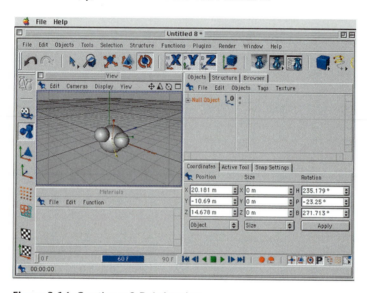

Figure 3.14 Creating a 3-D Animation

No matter which program you use, developing a 3-D animation is similar to creating two-dimensional animations. You create the objects, move them over time, and then save the file in the proper form. In Cinema 4D, the steps are as follows:

1. Create an object by clicking one from the list of 3-D shapes under the Objects menu. The object will appear at the center of the View window.

2. Create additional objects as necessary, and drag them in the x,y,z space in the View window to position them relative to the other objects.

3. Edit objects by changing their attributes under the Objects tab to the right of the View window.

4. Use the red keyframe button on the timeline under the View window to set the current position of the objects as the first frame of the animation.

5. Move the timeline to a future frame, such as frame 10.

6. In the View menu, click the Move button and then drag the x, y, or z axis to change the position of the objects.

7. Use the keyframe button again to define this new position as a keyframe.

8. Repeat steps 5, 6, and 7 to create additional movements and keyframes.

9. Preview the animation by using the controller buttons to the right of the timeline.

10. When the animation is finished, you must **render** it by clicking Render Settings from the Render menu. This action creates the intervening frames and adds the shading that gives the objects the impression of moving in 3-D space.

11. Use the Render Settings dialog box to set the size, frame rate, and other attributes of the animation.

12. Still in the Render Settings dialog box, use the Save tab to set the format of the file you will save. Cinema 4D can save in many formats, but only a few of them can be used directly in a Web page. The QuickTime Movie (`.mov`) format is the best choice here.

13. Use the Path button to assign a Web-legal filename, and save the file to the proper Web site folder.

14. Click Render to Picture Viewer in the Render menu.

15. Watch as Cinema 4D creates all intervening frames, with shading, and displays it in a window.

16. When the rendering is complete, you will find the animation file ready for embedding into a Web page.

☆ **DO IT YOURSELF** Use one or more of the approaches described here to create a simple animation and save it in a form suitable for a Web site.

As you can see, a high-quality animation requires many steps and lots of work. But the examples show only how the basic process works, barely scratching the surface of the possibilities of Web animation.

Embedding Animation in a Web Page

Now that you have created and saved the animation, you must place it in a Web page so that viewers can experience it. The method you use depends on the file format of the animation and on the tools you use to construct your Web pages. For a simple animated GIF, you use the same method as for still images, as described in Chapter Two. For Flash, QuickTime, and other file types that require plug-ins, you must embed them in the Web page using a different method.

Placing a GIF Animation in a Web Page

Because Web browsers treat animated GIFs in the same way they treat static GIF images, the same method and the same HTML code can be used. In a WYSIWYG editor such as Dreamweaver, follow these steps:

1. Place the pointer in the location you want the animation to appear. You can place it directly in the text of the page or in a table cell.

2. Click Image from the Insert menu.

3. Find the animation file you wish to place.

4. Click OK, and the first frame will appear on the page. The animation will remain static because Dreamweaver cannot display movement.

5. To see the animation at work in the page, click Preview in Browser from the File menu.

6. Observe the animation as it plays in the browser.

The HTML code for including a simple GIF animation looks like this:

```
<IMG SRC="media/bouncingball.gif">
```

Embedding Other Animations in a Web Page

Because Web browsers do not naturally recognize and display animations in the Flash (`.swf`) or QuickTime (`.mov`) format, these files use plug-ins. Any file that uses a plug-in must be **embedded** in the page using the HTML embed tag. To do this in a WYSIWYG editor such as Dreamweaver, follow these steps:

1. Place the pointer in the location you want the animation to appear. You can include it in the text of the page or in a table cell.

2. Click Media➜Plug-in from the Insert menu.

3. Find the animation file you wish to embed.

4. A square with a plug-in icon will appear at the location of the animation. You will not see the content of the animation because Dreamweaver cannot display plug-in animations.

5. Resize the square to match the size of your animation file.

6. To see the animation at work, click Preview in Browser from the File menu.

7. Observe the animation as it plays in the browser. Your browser must have the appropriate plug-in installed.

> ☆ **TIP   Identify the Plug-in**
>
> What if your site visitors don't have the plug-in to display the file you just embedded? It's a good idea to tell them where they can download it. Using a WYSIWYG editor such as Dreamweaver, enter the URL of the plug-in page (for example, the plug-in page for Shockwave is `http://www.macromedia.com/shockwave/download/`) in the Properties window of the embedded object. Or you can use the HTML attribute `pluginspage`, as shown in the code sample.

Here's the HTML code to embed a Flash animation:

```
<embed src="media/bouncingball.swf" width="320"
height="240" pluginspage="http://www.macromedia.com/
shockwave/download/"> </embed>
```

The HTML code to embed a QuickTime animation would look like this:

```
<embed src="media/bouncingball.mov" width="320"
height="240" pluginspage="http://www.apple.com/
quicktime/download/"> </embed>
```

☆**WARNING** With the embed tag, you must include the width and height of the animation or else it won't show on the page.

☆**DO IT YOURSELF**   Using the methods described here, place a GIF animation, and embed a Flash or QuickTime animation, in a Web page of your own. Test it with both Netscape and Explorer browsers to observe its performance.

☆**SHORTCUT**   Web addresses for the plug-ins are listed at the end of this chapter under Online References.

Most of your Web visitors will have little trouble viewing your GIF animations. The ability to interpret and display them is built into the Netscape and Internet Explorer browsers. Some users, however, may experience a time delay downloading a large animated GIF because of the file's size and bandwidth requirements.

Animations that require plug-ins raise additional issues. Both Flash and QuickTime plug-ins are free and widely distributed—they're included with most new computers and with most new browser packages—but some users may not have them installed or may have the file extensions improperly assigned in their browser preferences. Reinstalling the latest plug-in via download usually solves these problems.

☆**TIP**   **Installing Plug-ins**

Even though the Flash and QuickTime plug-ins are included with most new browser installations, many Web visitors will not have the latest version and may not have the plug-in properly configured. To install a plug-in, it must first be downloaded from its publisher's Web site. After they're downloaded, some plug-ins install themselves automatically, whereas others place an installer file on the desktop that must be double-clicked to begin installation. Most plug-in download sites provide a test page so that you can see whether the program is working correctly.

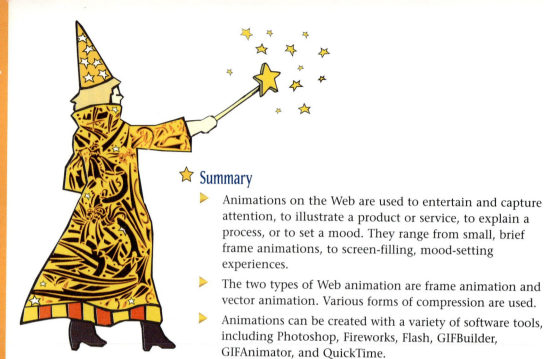

⭐ Summary

▶ Animations on the Web are used to entertain and capture attention, to illustrate a product or service, to explain a process, or to set a mood. They range from small, brief frame animations, to screen-filling, mood-setting experiences.

▶ The two types of Web animation are frame animation and vector animation. Various forms of compression are used.

▶ Animations can be created with a variety of software tools, including Photoshop, Fireworks, Flash, GIFBuilder, GIFAnimator, and QuickTime.

▷ Animated GIFs are placed on Web pages just as images are, whereas Flash and QuickTime animations must be embedded.

⭐ Online References

Flash and Shockwave plug-ins
http://www.macromedia.com/shockwave/download/

QuickTime plug-in
http://www.apple.com/quicktime/download/

Directory of Web browser plug-ins
http://www.netscape.com/plugins/

Macromedia Flash
http://www.macromedia.com/software/flash/

Macromedia Director Shockwave Studio
http://www.macromedia.com/software/director/

GIFBuilder
http://homepage.mac.com/piguet/gif.html

Microsoft GIF Animator
http://www.microsoft.com/frontpage/imagecomposer/imagecomposer5.htm

JASC Animation Shop
http://www.jasc.com/product.asp?pf%5Fid=003

Macromedia Fireworks
http://www.macromedia.com/software/fireworks/

Cinema 4D
http://www.maxoncomputer.com/

☆ Review Questions

1. How can animation help a Web site to achieve its objectives?

2. Explain the differences between frame animation and vector animation.

3. List the steps in preparing a frame animation for a Web site.

4. List the steps in preparing a vector animation for a Web site.

5. Describe at least three software programs that are used to create animations for the Web.

6. Which types of animation files require plug-ins for the Web browser?

7. List three advantages and three disadvantages of using animations that require a plug-in.

☆ Hands-On Exercises

1. Find on the Web an example of a site that uses animation to entertain or capture attention. Find another site where animation is used to explain a process. Find a third site where animation is used to set a mood. For each site, describe the nature of the animation and indicate whether you think it's a frame or vector animation.

2. Take a Web site that you are working on, or consider a hypothetical site, and draw up a plan for the use of animation on the site. For each animation that you propose, describe its purpose, its size, and what tools and resources would be needed to create it.

3. Use one of the software programs mentioned in this chapter to prepare a simple GIF animation. Include this animation in a simple Web page, and display it in a browser.

4. Use Flash or another vector animation program to prepare a more complex animation. Embed it in a Web page, and view it with a browser.

5. Visit the Web sites of three of the vendors of animation software programs listed above in the Resources section. View at least two of the showcase examples provided in each site. In each case, describe the nature of the animation, and its purpose.

CHAPTER FOUR

SOUND ON THE WEB

I n this chapter you'll learn about the possibilities and realities of using sound on the Web. You'll find out how the human voice, music, and sound effects can enhance the ways that a Web site communicates with its audience. You'll study how sound is digitized and compressed for the Web and learn about the technologies that are used to send and play it. You'll also find out how to record and edit sound and how to save it in formats suitable for embedding in a Web page.

Chapter Objectives

⭐ To learn the various ways that you can use voice, music, and sound effects to meet the aims of your Web site

⭐ To understand how sound works on the Web, including sampling, digitization, compression, and MIDI music, and to understand the difference between downloaded and streaming sound

To learn how to digitize, edit, and save sound files suitable for use on a Web site

 To discover how to embed sound in a Web page

The Possibilities of Sound on the Web

Sound is a newcomer to the Web. The Web began with text, later added images, and for most of its existence has been a silent medium for the typical viewer. But now sound is exploding on the Internet, especially with the emergence of MP3 files, streaming radio (streaming technology is discussed later), and new compression and playback technologies such as RealAudio and QuickTime.

> ☆TIP   **Sound Acronyms**
>
> AIFF (Audio Interchange File Format), MIDI (Musical Instrument Digital Interface), and WAV (waveform audio) are acronyms that describe various file formats for sound used on the Web. And MP3 is a shortened form of MPEG-3, which stands for Motion Picture Experts Group Number Three. The compression algorithms used to compress MP3 sound files originated in a scheme designed to compress the soundtracks of movie files.

Even after the tools for authoring Web sound were perfected, many sites did not include sound because of the bandwidth bottleneck discussed in Chapter One: Most home users with modems did not have a fast enough Internet connection to receive sound files with any degree of quality or speed.

So sound was at a standstill until two things happened: better bandwidth and better-crafted compression schemes. More homes, offices, and schools began to be connected with high-speed DSL, cable modem, or other methods that boosted bandwidths to acceptable levels for sending sound, and engineers invented new ways to compress sound into tiny files that still sounded good.

Types of Sounds on the Web

Imagine the Web site of the hypothetical Fred's Storm Door Company. The home page displays a smiling photo of Fred himself, and with a click of the mouse you hear him intone, "Hello, I'm Fred. Welcome to the best storm doors you'll ever open." If you click to the products page, you'll hear the solid sound of the latch on the Super Security model. You can browse Fred's online catalog to the music of Mozart (for aluminum doors) or Bach (wood doors). You can download step-by-step audio instructions for installing your own storm door. You can even download MP3 files of Fred's favorite groups, including The Doors, Raging Storm, The Latchkey Kids, and the BugScreens.

Fred's site doesn't exist, but it illustrates the many types of sound used on the Web. The human **voice** can greet you, remind you, explain a process, make a funny noise, or sing a song. **Music** can soothe the savage breast, excite the lovelorn, or create a somber mood. **Sound effects** can bring an image to life, respond to visitors, or add a touch of humor.

⭐**DO IT YOURSELF**   **Explore Sound**

Find sites on the Web that use all three types of sound: voice, music, and sound effects. What's the purpose of these sounds? How do they help accomplish the site's goals?

Sound can make a Web site seem like a radio station, a CD player, or a personal interview. By taking advantage of the communicative aspects of voice, music, and effects, a Web site can enhance its purposes and have an effect on the user that's impossible with text and images alone.

Voice

Some say that the voice was the first means of human communication. We used our voices to warn of danger and to teach our children. We learned to use our voices to tell stories. We recounted events that happened earlier, we foretold what might transpire in the future, and we composed parables that taught the meaning of right and wrong. Our spoken words soon overtook other forms of communication to become our favored method.

In addition to private and interpersonal communication, the human voice was used in small groups by gifted storytellers or in large crowds by civil and religious leaders. From Socrates to Cicero, those who mastered the technology of public speaking wielded great social influence. The master of the spoken word was the master of thought and reason.

Speech was powerful then, and it remains powerful today. Even after the emergence of the written word, the voice is an important form of communication. Powered by the force of their voices, Abraham Lincoln led the nation and Vladimir Lenin led a revolution. John F. Kennedy's Boston-accented voice remains as a legacy of his brief presidency, and the heartfelt words of Maya Angelou inspire and provoke us today to think and reflect in new ways. And more people today *hear* the news of the world than *read* it—the combined audience for TV and radio news far outnumbers the circulation of newspapers in the United States.

Voice is among the most ancient of instruments for communication, so it is fitting that we should use it on our Web sites. This chapter teaches you how the human voice can be digitized, edited, compressed, and embedded in a Web site.

Music

Long before the Beatles, INXS, and the Backstreet Boys found their way into the hearts and pocketbooks of the world's music lovers, human beings have realized the power of music to connect directly to our brains. Ancient forms of music—the rhythm of drums, the melody of the singing voice, and the harmony of people chanting in ensemble—were soon assembled to capture attention and communicate feelings and emotions. Later, we fashioned other instruments to extend our voices and our hands to produce sounds in all timbres and ranges.

In short, music has deep historical and psychological roots. It can set a mood, express anguish, celebrate success, or communicate romantic love. For these kinds of purposes, music seems to work better than words or pictures. Many of us, upon hearing only a few notes, can recall an entire piece or, even better, be transported back to the time and place when we first became familiar with the music. Music somehow drives deep into the mind and is remembered at a primitive level that seems closer to the gut than to the cerebrum.

We use music in our most fateful enterprises: Bagpipes, drums, and horns take us to war; violins accompany our intimate dinners; marches announce our weddings; dirges console our mourning. War, love, and death—each has its own music.

An effective Web site developer knows how to use music to help communicate ideas. Often used in combination with images and voices, music can reach the mind of the audience in ways not possible with other forms of communication.

<table>
<tr><td>

☆**DO IT YOURSELF**   **Consider Voice and Music**

How might voice or music help communicate a key idea in your Web site?

</td></tr>
</table>

Sound Effects

Sound is all around us: birds chirping, traffic blaring, wind blowing, glass shattering. These sound effects can form an unconscious backdrop to our daily affairs or a startling interruption to our train of thought. They can soothe, shock, please, or punish; they can bring on fear, suspense, happiness, or tension. When these same sounds are made part of a Web site, they have similar effects on visitors. The masters of film, theater, radio, and television production have learned to employ sound effects to great advantage. This same set of tools can enhance your Web site.

Stop for a moment and listen to the sound effects that surround you right now. How many can you identify? Which are natural? Which are of human origin? Which bother you? Which do you ignore? If you were planning a Web site, which of these sounds might you include?

☆**DO IT YOURSELF**   **Analyze Sounds**

Listen to the radio or watch television, and listen for sound effects. A good program for this is *Prairie Home Companion*, a radio show that makes extensive use of sound effects. It's on Saturday evenings on some public radio stations.

Using Sound on a Web Site

Sound can serve a variety of purposes on a Web site. It can convey information, set a mood, capture attention, explain a process, or provide a sense of personal contact.

Conveying Information

Click a word in the text, and hear it pronounced (see Figure 4.1). Click a product in the online catalog, and hear a short description of its benefits. Click on the picture of a motorcycle, and hear the throaty roar of its exhaust. Click the speaker icon, and listen to the story as it is read to you. In these examples, sound is used to provide important information in a direct and familiar way.

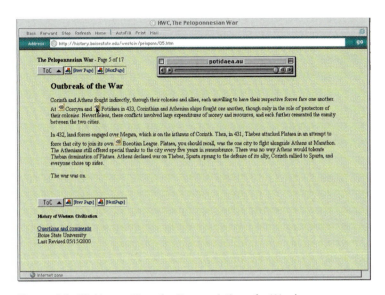

Figure 4.1 Clicking to Hear the Pronunciation of a Word

Setting a Mood

Listen to the birds sing as you browse the Nature Club site. Hear Mozart as you peruse the menu choices at the site of a French restaurant. Be rocked by an explosion as you enter the page describing the blow-out sale at Fred's Auto World. Listen to the soothing harmonies of a Gregorian chant as you view the Web page of the local monastery. The sounds in these sites are designed to change your mood and provide a context to help you understand the content of the site.

Capturing Attention

Hear the pop of a gun as you view the shoot-the-monkey banner ad. Listen to Fred's voice welcome you to his site. Hear the sound of clinking coins in the Web advertisement for a gambling site. These sounds, like the attention-getting animations described in Chapter Three, are intended to get you to pay attention to the advertisement or other item on display.

Explaining a Process

Listen to the instructor's voice in an online course explain how to place clip art into a PowerPoint slide. Hear the bank's loan officer recite the steps involved in borrowing money for a new car. Listen to the narrator tell a story that accompanies the pictures. We are accustomed to the human voice explaining such things in the real world, so it's natural to find these examples on Web sites.

Providing Personal Contact

A Web site can be a static, impersonal form of communication. Adding a voice, a laugh, a song, or a shout can make the site seem personal and intimate. Fred's voice welcoming you to his storm door company site, accompanied by a large portrait, can add a personal touch to an otherwise cold and commercial experience.

☆ **DO IT YOURSELF**   **Think About Sound**

Think of the Web site you're building. Which of the functions mentioned here might sound help you achieve? What kind of sound would be best? Where would it be included?

Notice that in some of these examples, the sound happens spontaneously; no user action is required. In others, the user must click to hear the sound. This distinction between **passive** and **active** sound on the Web is an important one, and you'll learn how to program both types later in this chapter.

How Sound Works on the Web

Sound, like all media on the Web, is digitized and saved in a file on the Web server. The sound file is embedded into or linked to a Web page, and it's downloaded to the visitor's computer just as an image or an animation file is. After it's downloaded, the file is either played automatically by the browser (passive mode), or played only when the user clicks a link (active mode). The only exception is **streaming** sound, in which the file plays as it arrives at the user's computer and is never actually downloaded to her disk.

You must create and save each sound for your site as a separate file, just as you prepared the image and animation files described in earlier chapters. The exception is **live streaming** sound. Here, no file is prepared in advance. Instead, you prepare a path from the audio-encoding **computer** to the streaming server and to the Web page. Streaming audio is explained later in this chapter.

Sound files for the Web come in two types: sampled sound and MIDI sound. These types are created and saved in two different ways, so they are treated separately here.

Sampled Sound

Most sound on the Web is **sampled** sound. MP3s, voices, songs, natural sound effects, and so on are recorded from real life, digitized, compressed, and saved in binary files as described in Chapter One.

In nature, sound is a continuous phenomenon that ranges smoothly over time without interruption. Think of an oboe playing a sustained note. Its sound persists, offering no natural breaks. A computer cannot handle such continuities. It can deal only with **discrete** numbers that can be divided up and counted. That's why it divides a photograph into pixels: It cannot store the image itself, but it can store the color and brightness of each pixel of the image.

The computer does a similar thing for sound. It divides the continuous tone into **samples**—for example, one sample taken every 44 thousandths of a second. This means that 44,000 times per second, the computer records the loudness and pitch of the sound that it hears. Just as the color and brightness of each pixel in an image are represented by numbers, the loudness and pitch of a sound are represented by numbers. The oboe plays into the microphone; the computer examines the signal coming from the microphone and samples the oboe music at a rate of 44 kilohertz (kHz).

Figure 4.2 displays the waveform from a sampled sound in the SoundEdit sound-editing program, showing how the process of sampling creates a data point for each split second of sound. The continuous sound wave has been divided into a series of discrete data points.

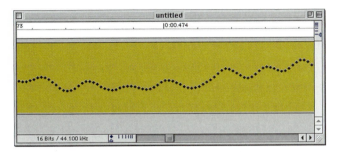

Figure 4.2 Sample Points in a Sound Waveform in SoundEdit

⭐**TIP   Kilohertz**

Heinrich Rudolf Hertz was a German scientist of the late nineteenth century who described the properties of electromagnetic waves and cycles. His name is used as the unit of measurement for frequency of these cycles in emissions such as sound and radio. 44 kilohertz (abbreviated kHz) means that the waves cycle 44,000 times per second.

This process of **digitization** (the French call it *numérisation*, probably a more accurate term) creates 44,000 numbers for each second of sound, each number consisting of 16 bits. This means that 10 seconds of sound—enough for Fred to welcome you to his Web site—would consume more than 7 million (7,000,000) bits of computer data.

Sampling Rate

Sound can be sampled at any rate you choose; the higher the rate, the more true-to-life the sound. The rate of 44 kHz is used for sampling the sound you hear on music CDs. Because most people can hear sounds only up to 22 kHz, using the 44 kHz rate—double the highest frequency we can hear—means that, for most people, the sampled sound is indistinguishable from the real thing.

Not all types of sound need such a high sampling rate to work well. The human voice can rarely produce sounds above 8 kHz, so there's no need to sample at a rate higher than 22 kHz. But for a symphony orchestra, with its many high-pitched sounds, you need a higher sampling rate to produce acceptable fidelity to the original music.

When sound is compressed, its sampling rate is often reduced. This reduces the amount of data but also lowers the quality of the sound. Compression methods for sound are discussed later in this chapter.

Any sound that your ear can hear can be sampled: birdsong, music, explosions, or voices. A microphone connected to the computer (or a device called a

digitizer—in reality, a special-purpose computer) converts the sound waves into an electrical signal, which the computer samples at the appropriate rate.

When the user plays the sampled sound from the Web site, the computer converts the string of numbers into a continuous electrical signal, which is sent along a wire to the speaker or headphones (see Figure 4.3). The speaker vibrates in time with the electrical signal, producing sound waves that travel through the air to the listener's ear. It's the opposite process of recording the sound.

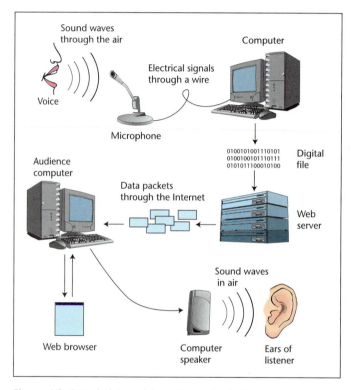

Figure 4.3 Sampled Sound from Source to Audience

☆ **DO IT YOURSELF**   **Sample Sound**

Use a sound-editing program or the built-in recorder on your computer to sample a sound from the real world. In Windows, the built-in recording utility is SoundRecorder. On Macintosh, it's SimpleSound. Save this sound on your hard disk. You'll use it later.

To be used in a Web site, a sampled sound must be digitized, edited, and saved in a suitable format. This process is described in the section Preparing Sound for the Web.

How Sound Works on the Web

MIDI Sound

MIDI, the other format, is a method for representing sounds produced by electronic musical instruments. Compared with sampled sound, MIDI files are much smaller and so transmit faster—much faster—over the Internet. I have a MIDI recording of a Mozart rondo that's 3 minutes, 44 seconds long. It takes up 19K. I have the same piece saved as a lower-quality sampled sound, and it takes 38MB. That's 2000 times bigger! Even with maximum compression, the sampled file size would remain at 655K, or 34 times bigger than the MIDI file.

How can the MIDI system result in such small files? MIDI was designed to record and save songs played by electronic musical instruments, also known as MIDI instruments. These instruments, when played, do not produce audible sounds; instead, they produce a sequence of numbers that represent the note that's being played (such as C-sharp), its loudness, the length of time, and the type of instrument. So playing a B-flat on a MIDI oboe produces four numbers that indicate the pitch (B-flat), the volume (say, 134 on a 255-point scale), the duration (2 seconds), and the instrument (an oboe). So it takes only 3 bytes of data to represent these 2 seconds of sound rather than the 88,000 bytes that might be needed for a sampled sound of the same oboe.

You can think of a MIDI file as containing the same information that's conveyed by sheet music—one data point for each note, telling the musician (or the computer) the pitch of the note, its duration, and any special effects that should be applied to it.

The string of numbers, in digital form, is sent from the MIDI instrument over a wire to the **synthesizer**. This device transforms the numbers into sounds you can hear and play through a speaker, or saves the numbers into a MIDI file on the synthesizer's memory or disk.

Or the numbers can be sent in digital form from the MIDI instrument to a computer, which can do one of three things:

 transform the numbers into sounds you can hear and play through a speaker;

 save the numbers into a MIDI file on the computer's disk; or

 display and record the numbers in a program called a **sequencer**. This device lets you combine and edit MIDI sounds to produce a multipart performance, which is then saved as a MIDI file.

These MIDI files can be used in a Web site and then converted into audible sound by the appropriate plug-in. Figure 4.4 shows the process of producing, saving, and playing MIDI music to a Web audience.

> ☆ **TIP**   **Analog-to-Digital Transformation**
>
> Your ear can't hear numbers, only sound waves. For you to hear a digital sound file, consisting only of discrete numbers, it must be transformed to the analog, "real-life" form of continuous waves. This is called an **analog-to-digital** transformation, sometimes abbreviated A to D or A/D. The opposite transformation—a D to A conversion—occurs when analog sound is sampled and digitized.

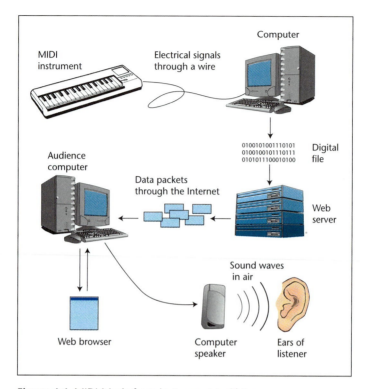

Figure 4.4 MIDI Music from Instrument to Listener

When the MIDI file arrives at the user's computer as part of your Web site, it is interpreted by a plug-in such as QuickTime Player, which uses the digital-to-analog circuitry of your computer to play the file through the speaker or headphones. The plug-in serves as a synthesizer, re-creating the sounds of the various instruments from the MIDI code it receives. With good speakers and a high-quality plug-in, the music can be of room-filling quality. But not all Web users have installed the plug-in that gives them MIDI capability. Before including MIDI music in your site, be sure to understand the computing situation of your typical visitor.

☆ **SHORTCUT**   The Online References section lists some sources for ready-made music.

If you're a musician you can make your own MIDI files, or you can find them ready-made from a variety of sources, ranging from MIDI collections on CD to free downloads from a Web site. No matter what the source, you must prepare the MIDI music for use in a Web page, as described in the next section. MIDI files must be saved in the proper format, but they do not need to be compressed.

☆ **DO IT YOURSELF**   **Make MIDI Music**

Work with MIDI music by creating your own files from a MIDI instrument or MIDI sequencing software, or by downloading MIDI files from the Web. Listen to the files, note their small sizes, and choose one or two for inclusion in a Web site you're working on.

Because of their small size, MIDI files can include by far the most music for the least download time. But MIDI can be used only for music and not for voice. And because of the way it's constructed, you can't convert existing analog music to the MIDI format: MIDI files can be created only by MIDI instruments or sequencers. MIDI is a good choice for long passages of music designed to create a mood on your site.

Compression Methods

The technology for the compression of sampled sounds is moving forward very quickly. The growth of the Web (and of digital cell phones) has created a great demand for software that can compress and decompress a digitized sound file quickly. Digital mobile phones do this, as does your computer. They both contain codecs (see Chapter One) that turn the compressed data into acceptable audible sound. In fact, some of the same codec technology is used in phones and in computers.

Chapter One explains data compression in general. To compress sound files, the following techniques are used.

Repetition and Patterns

Consider the oboe playing a note for two seconds. The numbers that represent the pitch and loudness of the sound would be pretty much the same over those two seconds. So instead of saving the same number 88,000 times, the codec records it once and then adds "ditto, 79,999 more times." This saves an extraordinary amount of data. But it works this well only for simple sounds that have little variation, and few sounds on a Web site will contain such sustained oboe playing. Still, all sound includes some repetition that the codec can work with.

Sound also contains patterns—sequences of identical sound—that occur repeatedly in the file. A sophisticated codec can look through the numbers and identify these patterns. It records the pattern once and then assigns a single number, sometimes called a **token**, to represent it. As the codec compresses the file, it replaces all the bits of the pattern with the token, saving even more space. Done well, repetition and patterning loses very little information and thus has very little effect on the quality of the sound after it's been decompressed.

Averaging

Just as the JPEG image-compression algorithm groups neighboring pixels of similar color and averages them into a single number, a sound-compression codec can average groups of data points that sound almost the same, saving one number for every 4 or 8 or 16 data points. This reduces the amount of data in the file but causes some degradation in fidelity.

Selectivity

Not all sounds are perceived equally by the human ear. We are highly sensitive to certain parts of the sound spectrum, but for others we don't notice the difference between pitches that are close together. A good codec takes into account our selective hearing and does more averaging (and looser pattern matching) with those sounds that we don't discriminate well. In this way, the amount of data can be reduced without a noticeable loss.

Range Reduction

Most sound that we hear has a wide dynamic range; there's quite a difference between the softest note (or quietest whisper) and the loudest crescendo (or shouted voice). When sound is digitized, this range is recorded on a scale—for example, from 1 to 255, soft to loud. So it takes an 8-bit number to represent it. Reducing the scale so that the loudest sound is 64 and the softest 1, the codec can use a 6-bit number, thus reducing the amount of data needed. This reduction in range is noticeable, but only to the practiced ear and only in certain kinds of sound. The same principle can be applied selectively to certain pitches to which the human ear is less sensitive.

Modern codecs apply all these compression methods, and others are being invented as this book is written. Web developers use many different codecs; your choice depends on which ones your sound-editing software offers, and which ones your audience is likely to have installed. Remember that any codec you use must be present to decompress the file on the visitor's computer.

You specify the method and extent of compression when you save the sound file in your sound-editing program. This process is described in the next section.

☆DO IT YOURSELF   Compress Sound

Using one of the sound-editing software programs mentioned in this chapter, compress a sampled sound with different methods and extents, listen to the differences, and note the resulting file sizes.

Downloading versus Streaming

There are two ways to send a sound file to your Web site audience: download it to their hard drive or stream it to them. Most small sound files are downloaded from the Web server just as image files are. But some larger files are streamed. Streaming is more complex, for both the server and the user, but it offers certain advantages. You would use streaming audio under these conditions:

 You are presenting live events. The only way to let listeners hear an event in real time, as it's being spoken or played, is to stream the sound. In streaming, the user hears the sound as soon as the sound data is reassembled and decompressed by his computer.

 The sound requires very large files. When a file is downloaded to a user, it resides on his hard disk. Many Web users will not have sufficient disk space to hold more than a few downloads of lengthy music or sound files.

 You need to save download time. A popular song might be compressed from 25MB on a CD to 4 or 5 megabytes. But even at this size, typical modem users would wait more than 10 minutes for it to download before listening. Streaming the same song lets them hear it after only a few seconds.

 You need to secure your files from being copied. A downloaded audio file, residing on the user's hard disk, can be copied and shared with others over a network or on homemade CDs. A streamed file is not copied to the user's disk and thus cannot be copied or shared.

You need to conserve bandwidth. Suppose your Web site includes a recording of the company president's quarterly address to stockholders. If many stockholders download the file at the same time, the server must set up a separate communication session with each one, devoting considerable bandwidth to this task. But if you set up a live **multicast** stream, only one instance of the transmission is sent; any number of people can tap into the stream and receive the file.

To stream a file to a public audience, you must set up a **streaming server**: special software run on a Web server that sends the stream to your audience and monitors its reception by each user. A streaming server can contain **archived streaming files**—prerecorded sound files saved in a special format on the server's hard disk that any user can access at any time—or **live streams**, which can be accessed only in real time, as they are happening. Figure 4.5 shows how this works.

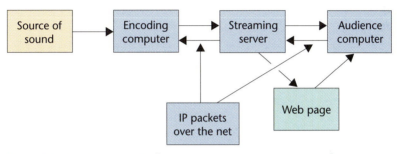

Figure 4.5 Live Streaming Audio

Whether the file is live or archived, the streaming server sets up a separate Internet connection, called a **session**, with each listener. The server **packetizes** the sound data—forms it into standard Internet packets of data—and sends a stream of packets to each user. Packets that get lost along the way are re-sent as necessary. When the packets arrive at the user's computer, they are reassembled into the correct order, decompressed, and then played through the computer's speaker or headphones.

In a multicast stream, the **encoding computer**—the one connected to the microphone that's picking up the live event—sends a single stream of packets containing the audio data. This single stream, called a **broadcast**, can then be picked up by multiple users.

In a multicast stream, the packet headers do not contain the IP address of the intended recipient because they're intended for multiple recipients. Because of the lack of this header information, many Internet routers do not let multicast packets pass through. So a multicast is best used in a local area network where all the routers are multicast-enabled, as in a large corporation or school.

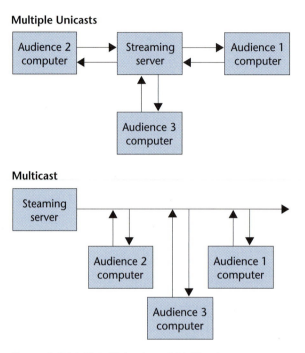

Figure 4.6 Multiple Unicasts and Multicast

Streaming servers that can handle audio include the QuickTime streaming server from Apple Computer; the RealServer from RealNetworks; and the Windows Media Server from Microsoft. For originating live streams for these servers, encoding software includes Sorenson Broadcaster, RealProducer, and Windows Media Encoder. Online information sources for these products are listed in the References section.

File Formats for Sound

Sound on the Web is found in many different file formats, as indicated by the extensions `.aif`, `.au`, `.mov`, `.mid`, `.mp3`, `.wav`, `.ram`, `.asf`, and others. Each of these formats stores its data in a unique way, and each requires a plug-in to play the file. As with image file formats, each sound format was invented by a different, often competing, organization for a different purpose. Table 4.1 shows some of the most common formats, their origins, and their uses on the Web.

Table 4.1 Sound File Formats

Filename Extension	Origin	Web Use
.aif	Audio Interchange File Format, designed as a common audio format among programs and platforms	Limited current use on the Web.
.au	UNIX audio file format	Most early Web audio was in this format, and it's still used.
.mov	QuickTime format, originated by Apple, used for both video and sound	Widely used for embedded and linked sound and video.
.mid	MIDI file	Can be interpreted by QuickTime and other plug-ins.
.ram	RealAudio streaming format from RealNetworks	Widely used for streaming audio. Needs RealPlayer plug-in.
.asf	Windows Media Player format	Newcomer to the Web audio scene.
.wav	Waveform audio file format	Early DOS-Windows audio format, still used extensively.
.mp3	Audio track from MPEG-3 compression scheme	Widely used for popular music tracks. Can be interpreted by QuickTime and other plug-ins.

The choice of file format depends on several factors:

 The nature of the sound

 The way you plan to embed the sound in your site

 The plug-ins your audience is likely to have

⭐ The type of sound-editing software you use

⭐ The kind of streaming server that your organization uses

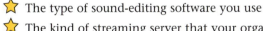

◎๏ Preparing Sound for the Web

Each sound that you plan to use on your Web site must be prepared and saved separately. To do this, you need a computer with sound-digitizing (analog-to-digital) circuitry as well as sound-capture and -editing software. Most modern multimedia computers sold today have the circuitry built-in, but few include the software. The software lets you capture the sound from its source, modify and mix it, compress it, and save it in a suitable format.

Hardware Requirements

To capture and digitize sound from analog (natural) sources, you need a sound input device such as a microphone; a sound input connector on the computer; and analog-to-digital circuitry inside the computer. The diagram in Figure 4.7 shows how this works.

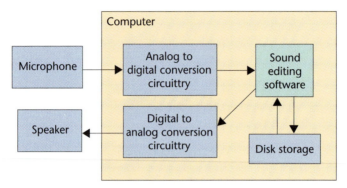

Figure 4.7 Sound Recording Hardware Setup

Two systems are used to connect the microphone to the computer: line input and USB. The **line input** connector accepts standard microphones such as those used with tape recorders and sound systems and is usually in the form of a one-eighth-inch diameter stereo mini plug. Line input receives an analog electrical signal from the microphone and passes it to the computer's analog-to-digital converter circuitry. On many computers, the microphone is built in to the computer case itself and needs no external connection or device.

A **Universal Serial Bus (USB)** connector takes a USB microphone. This mike sends digital data to the USB port on the computer, which connects directly to the computer's data bus.

The computer needs adequate disk space to store the sound data it receives, as well as speakers or headphones to play the sound back to the editor. A fast hard disk is essential because media such as floppy and Zip disks cannot deliver sound data to the computer fast enough for high-quality editing.

Software Tools

Many software tools are available for capturing, editing, and saving sound for a Web site. Professional sound-editing systems used in the recording industry sell for several thousand dollars; simple built-in sound recorder utilities are part of the computer's operating system.

Complete preparation calls for software tools that can perform these functions:

 Capture the sound from a microphone, tape player, music CD, or other source.

 Display the sound on the screen in a form that makes it easy to edit. Most editors use a waveform pattern in a window.

⭐ Edit the sound by manipulating the display, making changes, cutting, copying, and pasting.

⭐ Combine sounds from several sources in parallel **tracks** that can be edited separately, played back together, and coordinated.

⭐ Apply effects to the sound, or parts of it, ranging from echoes to amplification to reverberation.

⭐ Mix various tracks into a single sound file.

⭐ Compress and save the file in a variety of formats with a variety of codecs.

Few software packages can do all these things well, so you often must use several tools to prepare the sound. Table 4.2 lists some of the common software tools.

Table 4.2 Software for Preparing Sound Files

Software	Platform	Capture	Display	Edit	Combine Tracks	Effects	Mix	Compress	Save File Formats
SoundRecorder	Windows	yes	yes	yes	no	no	no	no	`.wav` only
SimpleSound	Macintosh	yes	no	no	no	no	no	no	`.snd` only
SoundEdit	Macintosh	**yes***	**yes**	**yes**	**yes**	**yes**	**yes**	no	`.mov`, `.aif`, `.wav`
Sound Forge	Windows	**yes**	yes	yes	no	**yes**	yes	yes	All Web formats
CoolEdit Pro	Windows	yes	**yes**	**yes**	**yes**	yes	yes	yes	All Web formats
QuickTime Pro Player	Windows and Macintosh	no	no	limited	yes	no	yes	**yes**	**All Web formats**
Flash	Windows and Macintosh	no	yes	limited	yes	limited	yes	yes	`.swf`, `.mov`

* Particular strengths of certain tools are shown in boldface.

SoundRecorder and SimpleSound are included as part of the operating system at no extra cost on Windows and Macintosh computers, respectively. The others range from about $30 for QuickTime Player Pro to several hundred dollars for Flash, SoundEdit, Soundforge, and CoolEdit Pro.

⭐**DO IT YOURSELF   Are You Equipped for Sound?**

Examine your computer hardware and software. Is it equipped to prepare sound for the Web? Does it have circuitry, commonly known as a **sound card**, to digitize analog sound? Does it have a microphone and speakers (or headphones)? Which sound-editing software (if any) is available? Does it work? This inspection will get you ready to capture, edit, and save sound for the Web.

Digitizing and Editing Sampled Sound

To prepare a sound for the Web, you must first set up your hardware and software, then capture the sound from its source, edit it, and finally compress and save it in a suitable format. The process is similar for most of the software packages listed in Table 4.2. We'll use SoundEdit to illustrate the steps.

Set Up the System

Install or locate the software, connect the microphone or other input device, and launch the software. To test whether the sound is coming through, speak into the microphone and look for your voice in the sound level meter. If no sound is coming through, check the system software Sound control panel to make sure that the microphone is selected as the input source. This control panel may also let you set the volume of the input device.

> ★ **SHORTCUT**   Test your sound system in an isolated, quiet space, with good headphones. It makes the process easier and produces better results.

When you can see the sound in the level meter, make a test recording. Click the Record button, speak into the microphone, and then click the Stop button. Then click the Play button to hear the sound. Figure 4.8 shows what these buttons look like in SoundEdit.

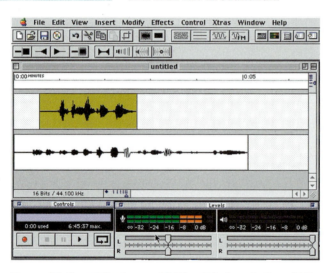

Figure 4.8 Sound Capture and Editing Windows in SoundEdit

Capture the Sound

Sound can be brought into the editor from the analog world through a microphone or tape player; or from the digital world of music CDs or music data files. To capture sound from an analog source, follow these steps:

1. Check the level. Say a few words or play the tape, and watch the sound level indicator. It should reach the top at the loudest parts of the sound and stay above the middle for most of the sound. Adjust the input level until you reach this result.

2. Secure the microphone. Don't hold it in your hand, something that introduces noise from your fingers. Put it on a stand, or clamp it to the computer monitor so that you can speak into it easily.

3. Record the sound. Click the Record button, speak or play, and then click the Stop button. As you speak, talk over or around the microphone, not directly into it. This will avoid **plosive** (concussive) p's and b's caused by your breath being picked up by the mike.

4. Look at the sound displayed in the editing window. It should look like the waveform in Figure 4.8. If it looks like the one on the top in Figure 4.9, it's too soft. If it looks like the one on the bottom, it's too loud.

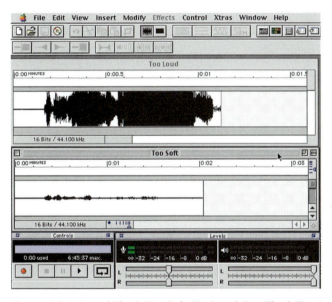

Figure 4.9 A Sound That's Too Soft (Top) and One That's Too Loud

5. Listen to the sound. Click the Play button to hear what you have recorded. Listen for clarity and quality.

6. Repeat this process until you get it right.

To capture sound that's in digital form, such as music CD tracks or an existing music file, follow these steps:

1. Click the Import or Convert item from the editor's menu bar, and navigate to the track or file that you want to capture.

2. If it's a track from a music CD, click the Options button to make a selection from the track; rarely will you want to include an entire 25MB track on your Web site. In SoundEdit, you can also set the sampling rate and bit depth in the Options window.

3. Look at the sound's waveform in the editing window.

4. Evaluate the sound by clicking the Play button, listening for quality and clarity.

Edit the Sound

Now you can go to work on the waveform that you see in the editing window. You can, for example, select a piece of sound and cut it, or copy and then paste it. You can fade in the beginning and fade out the end so that the sound does not start or stop abruptly. In SoundEdit, you select the target portion of the waveform and then click Fade out from the Effects menu.

Combine Sounds

Many editors let you work with several tracks at the same time. One track might contain background music, another narration, and a third sound effects of applause. You can coordinate these over time so that they blend to create a sound experience similar to that of a radio commercial. Figure 4.8 shows the separate tracks in the SoundEdit document window. Here's how to add a track and coordinate it with SoundEdit.

⭐ Add a second track to the editing window by clicking Insert Track from the Insert menu.

⭐ Import a sound into this track. It can come from a live source or from an existing file. The two tracks are displayed in parallel on the display, as shown in Figure 4.8.

⭐ To move one track along the timeline, press the Option key and drag with the mouse.

⭐ To apply an effect to one track only, select it and choose the effect from the Effects menu. To apply the same effect to both tracks, click Select All from the Edit menu, and then apply the effect.

⭐ To mix both tracks into one, select them both and then click Mix from the Effects menu.

Apply Effects

The effects you can create with software such as SoundEdit range from the sublime to the ridiculous. You can amplify or attenuate the sound. You can make it play faster or slower. You can change the pitch to make normal adults sound like the Chipmunks or children sound like Dracula. You can add an echo or a reverberation. You can make it play backward, or you can filter out the high (or low) elements of the sound. To apply effects, follow these steps:

1. Select the target portions of the sound by clicking and dragging over it.

2. Choose the effect you want from the Effects menu.

3. Set the parameters for the effect, if necessary.

4. Apply the effect.

5. Listen to the results.

6. If it's not right, immediately click Undo from the Edit menu.

★TIP   Keep It Simple

A sound file with too many effects, such as reverberation, echo, amplitude changes, and pitch changes, may be disconcerting as well as difficult to listen to. Use only those effects that you need to get your idea across.

Mix the Tracks

If the sound consists of more than one track, you must mix it into a single track before it can be compressed and saved for the Web. Select all the tracks by clicking Select All from the Edit menu; then click Mix from the Effects menu to combine the tracks into one.

Compress and Save

Next, you save the file in a suitable file format and compress it so that it travels efficiently over the Internet. If the sound is to be streamed from a streaming server, you save it in the server's specific streaming format using a special software program such as RealProducer, QuickTime Player Pro, or Windows Media Encoder. If the sound is simply to be downloaded to users, you can save it in whichever format works best for your audience and for the type of sound. See Table 4.1 for a list of possible file formats.

In SoundEdit and most other editing programs, click Save or Export from the File menu to open the file saving dialog box. This dialog box gives you options for saving in terms of file type and perhaps in terms of the codec used for compression. Files saved in `.aif`, `.mov`, or `.wav` format can be received by most Web visitors.

The most compression for the least loss in quality will result from the Qualcomm Purevoice codec (for sounds that are mostly voice) or from the Q Design Music codec (if the sound is mostly music). These codecs are not available in SoundEdit, our sample editing program. To use these codecs in SoundEdit, you save the file first in `.mov` (QuickTime) format, open the `.mov` file with QuickTime Player Pro, and then export it with the desired codec.

★DO IT YOURSELF   Edit Sound

Use a software program such as SoundEdit, SoundForge, or CoolEdit Pro to edit sampled sound and prepare it for use on a Web site.

Other Ways to Edit Sound

If you do not have a full-featured sound-editing program such as SoundEdit or CoolEdit Pro, you can still capture sound and perform rudimentary sound editing by combining your computer's built-in sound recording utilities with other programs such as Flash or QuickTime Player Pro. The process is not as smooth, the possibilities are fewer, and the results not as good, but in a pinch it can work. Here's how.

Capture the Sound

The first step is to capture the sound. With Windows, use the SoundRecorder utility, usually located in the Multimedia control panel. On Macintosh, use the SimpleSound utility, located in the Apple Extras folder. Click New from the File menu to see a controller that looks like Figure 4.10.

Figure 4.10 Sound Recording Control Panel on Macintosh

The curved lines to the right of the speaker indicate the volume of the incoming sound. Click the Record button, speak, and then click the Stop button. Click the Play button to hear what you've just recorded. Click the Save button to save the file.

To record from a music CD, you can use this same method except that you use the computer's Sound control panel to switch the sound input from microphone to CD player. Use the computer's audio CD player software to stop and start the music; then use the sound recording utility to record the portion you need.

The sound files that you've saved are unedited and uncompressed, so they're not yet suitable for inclusion in a Web page. You must open them with another program that can compress and save them in the proper format.

Edit and Compress the Sound

Among the widely available programs you can use to edit and compress your sound files are QuickTime Player Pro and Flash. Although they aren't designed for this purpose, they can do the job.

To use QuickTime Player Pro, click Open Movie from the File menu to open the sound file you just recorded. Click the Play button to hear it. At this point, you can perform simple cut, copy, and paste editing by dragging the selection triangles along the progress indicator bar, as shown in Figure 4.11. The portion of the sound between the triangles is selected and can be copied or cut. You can even add additional tracks: Copy the sound from one QuickTime Player window, then moving to the other window, pressing the Option key and clicking Add from the Edit menu.

When your sound is edited and ready to save, click Export from the File menu, and then choose from among the many options for file format and codec. You choose the file format from the pop-up Export menu, and choose the codec and compression parameters by clicking the Options button. Many settings are accessible via the Settings button. For the Web, choose QuickTime movie, AIF, or Wave as the file format. Under settings, choose as follows:

 If the sound is mostly voice, choose the Qualcomm PureVoice codec at 22 kHz sampling, 16-bit mono.

⭐ If the sound is mostly music, choose the Q Design Music codec at 22 kHz sampling, 16-bit mono or stereo.

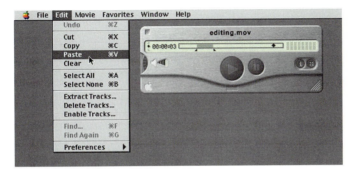

Figure 4.11 Editing Sound in QuickTime Player Pro

These codecs apply many compression techniques and result in small files. But you can also experiment with others in the list. As you save the file, make sure the filename extension matches the file format that you chose.

To use Flash, create a new Flash movie. Insert a new layer. Click Import from the File menu to bring in the sound that you recorded and saved earlier. Double-click the first frame of the layer to bring up its Properties window, and then choose the Sound tab and select the sound from the pop-up menu. The sound is now in that layer. Add a keyframe in frame 20 of that layer to give the sound room to play. You will see its waveform in the layer. Click Play on the controller to hear the sound.

You can create multiple tracks by creating new layers and importing a different sound into each one. To edit the sound with fade-in and fade out and adjust the volume, open the layer's Properties window and choose the Sound tab.

When the sound is complete, choose Export Movie from the File menu. For the Web, you can save this sound as a QuickTime movie (`.mov`) or as a Flash Player movie (`.swf`). As you save, you can set the sampling rate and bit depth. Use 11 kHz, 16-bit mono for voice, and 22 kHz, 16-bit mono or stereo for music. Saving in the Flash movie format compresses the file more than saving in the QuickTime movie format.

Preparing MIDI Music

MIDI music is not sampled, so it can't be edited with the standard sound-editing software tools. (You can convert a MIDI file to a sampled file and then edit it as described earlier, but this will increase its size more than a hundredfold and eliminate the benefits of the MIDI format.) To prepare a MIDI file for use on the Web, open it with QuickTime Pro player, click Save As from the File menu, and save it as a self-contained file with the extension `.mov`. Now you can perform simple cut-and-paste editing with QuickTime Player Pro, as described earlier. You can even add tracks (including sampled tracks) by copying them from another QuickTime player window and pressing the Option key as you click Add from the Edit menu.

The `.mov` file that you saved contains the MIDI data, but it's in a format that can pass easily through Web servers and play easily in browsers equipped with the QuickTime plug-in, all the while maintaining the small size and high quality of the MIDI format. Saving in this `.mov` format also allows you to use the full set of QuickTime playback parameters when you embed the sound into your Web page.

⭐ **DO IT YOURSELF**   **Edit More Sound**

Work with the other editing systems, such as Flash, QuickTime Player Pro, and MIDI, to prepare and export a sound for your Web site.

Filenames, Formats, and Directories

It's essential that the filename extensions of your sound file match the format you saved them in and that they are saved in the proper directory (folder) for your Web site. Remember that the filenames must also be Web-legal, containing no spaces, slashes, capital letters, or special characters.

Many Web developers set up a directory called `media` into which they place all the images, animations, sounds, and videos for the site. Other developers set up a directory for each type of medium. Make sure all your files are properly named and saved in the correct directory.

Formats for Streaming Sound

Streaming sound must be compressed and saved in the special format demanded by the streaming server. For the QuickTime streaming server, you must add a **hinted streaming track**: Open the file in QuickTime Player Pro, and export it in the Hinted Movie format. For the RealNetworks server, you use the RealProducer program to open the file and save it in the proprietary RealAudio format. For the Windows Media server, prepare the file with the Windows Media Encoder program, and save it in the streaming format.

These files must be saved on the streaming server, which may be in a different place from the rest of your Web site. Your organization's Web master can arrange for you to access the proper directory on the streaming server so that you can save the files.

⭐ **DO IT YOURSELF**   **Edit Sound**

Use one or more of the methods described here to capture, edit, and save some sounds for your Web site. Even if you don't have a full-fledged sound editor, you can use the rudimentary method to create some files to work with.

Including Sound on a Web Page

Now that you have prepared your sounds, you must make them a part of your Web site. Sounds can be embedded in a Web page, just as images and animations are, so that their representation displays directly on the page; or they can be linked to a Web page and display in their own separate window.

> **⭐ WARNING Unsolicited Sound**
>
> It may not be wise or appropriate to play a sound automatically on a Web page without giving users any means to control it or turn it off. Some visitors may be working in a quiet place where the sound will be a disturbance.

Embedding provides a smoother viewer experience and lets you integrate the sound more carefully with the other page elements. It also lets you play a sound in the background, with no visual interruption; and the developer can set certain user control parameters to control how the sound plays.

Linking sets up a separate browser window for the sound, and this window can be manipulated by the user independently from the rest of the content of the page.

Embedding Sound Using a WYSIWYG Web Page Editor

Embedding sound on a Web page using an editor such as Dreamweaver is very similar to inserting an image. Follow these steps:

1. Place the pointer at the location where you want the sound to play. (If it is to be a hidden background sound, place the pointer at the top of the page, before the other items.)

2. From the Insert menu, click Media and then click Plug-in because sound requires a plug-in.

3. In the file section dialog box, choose the desired sound file from the proper directory. A square with the plug-in icon appears in the document window at the pointer location. This square represents the sound.

4. If you plan to display a controller bar, stretch the square to the length and height of the controller, such as 16 pixels high and 128 pixels wide.

5. Preview the page in the browser to test the sound. (The default setting for embedded sound is to play it as soon as the page loads and to display the controller.)

Embedding Sound Using HTML

To embed a sound with HTML, use this code:

```
<embed src="/media/test.mov" width="128"
height="16"></embed>
```

The name of the sound file is `test.mov`, and it's in the `media` directory. The controller will display at 16 pixels high and 128 pixels wide.

Parameters for Embedded Sound

To control the way that sound is played and controlled by the user, you can set **parameters** for an embedded sound when you insert the sound. These parameters send instructions to the browser and the plug-in about how the sound should be played. In a WYSIWYG editor such as Dreamweaver, you set the parameters by selecting the square plug-in icon and opening its Properties window; then you click the Parameters button (see Figure 4.12).

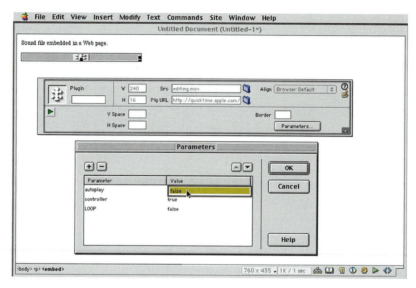

Figure 4.12 Setting Sound Parameters in Dreamweaver

Table 4.3 shows some of the parameters you can set.

Table 4.3 Parameters for Controlling Sound

Parameter	Values	Result
Autoplay	True or false	Plays the sound as soon as the page is viewed
Controller	True or false	Shows a slider that lets the user stop, start, advance, or rewind the sound
Height	Measurement in pixels	Sets the height of the controller
Hidden	True or false	Hides the file so that no visual indication is displayed
Loop	True or false	Plays the sound repeatedly
Width	Measurement in pixels	Sets the width of the controller

To use a sound as a background that begins playing as soon as the page is loaded, has no visual representation on the screen, and plays repeatedly, set the hidden parameter to true, controller to false, and autoplay to true. Also set width and height to zero. Such a sound in HTML code would look like this:

```
<embed src="/media/test.mov" width="0" height="0"
autoplay="true" hidden="true" loop="true"></embed>
```

Use a WYSIWYG editor or HTML code to embed a sound in a Web page. Test it in the Netscape and the Internet Explorer browsers. Then adjust the various parameters and observe changes in the sound's behavior.

Linking Sound Using a WYSIWYG Editor

You would use a linked sound when you want your audience to click a word in the text and hear it pronounced or you want them to click a hot spot in an image and hear a sound. A link is often used to make a connection to a RealNetworks streaming audio that opens in the RealPlayer window. Any form of sound can be linked; when the link is clicked, the sound file opens in a separate window.

To link a sound from a Web page, follow these steps.

1. Choose the item you wish to link from. It can be a word or phrase in the test, a button, an image, or a hot spot in an image map.

2. Click Make Link from the Modify menu.

3. Click the folder icon, and then navigate to the sound file in the file selection dialog box.

4. Click OK, and the link is made.

5. Test the link by previewing the page in a Web browser.

The nature of the window that displays the sound will depend on the plug-in that's used to play the sound. QuickTime uses a plain window with a simple controller bar. RealPlayer opens a large window with advertising and progress indicators.

Linking Sound Using HTML

Here's the HTML code to link to a sound from a Web page:

```
Here is the <a href="/media/test.mov">link</a>
```

In this example, `link` makes a link to the sound file `test.mov` in the `media` directory. Notice that this is the same code that's used to link to any other URL on the Web.

Use a WYSIWYG editor or HTML code to link to a sound from a Web page. Test it in both browsers.

Providing User Control

Sound offers great possibilities to enhance a Web site and fulfill its purposes. But it also harbors dangerous pitfalls. Think carefully about your audience before you include sound in your Web site. Consider these questions:

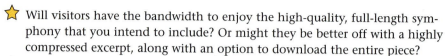
⭐ Will visitors have the bandwidth to enjoy the high-quality, full-length symphony that you intend to include? Or might they be better off with a highly compressed excerpt, along with an option to download the entire piece?

⭐ Should the sound be hidden, automatic, and uncontrollable by the user and simply play as the page opens? Or should you provide a controller so that users can stop, start, and repeat the sound as desired?

⭐ Should you embed the sound in the page and place its controller next to the text or image that accompanies it? Or should you open the sound in its own window and risk some confusion as the window opens in front of the Web page and covers its contents?

⭐ On a menu page that users will keep returning to, is it wise to include a sound that plays automatically? Will they get tired of hearing Fred's voice welcome them to the site each time they return to the main menu?

⭐ Will your audience have the patience to wait for your 5MB sound file to download? Might you be better off to compress it so that the wait is more reasonable?

When in doubt about how to include sound in a Web page, it's best to err on the side of user control. Let your audience decide how, when, and where to listen to the sound. And be courteous—let them turn it off if they'd rather not listen.

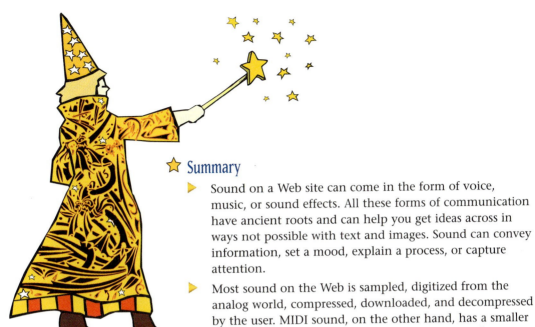

☆ Summary

▷ Sound on a Web site can come in the form of voice, music, or sound effects. All these forms of communication have ancient roots and can help you get ideas across in ways not possible with text and images. Sound can convey information, set a mood, explain a process, or capture attention.

▷ Most sound on the Web is sampled, digitized from the analog world, compressed, downloaded, and decompressed by the user. MIDI sound, on the other hand, has a smaller file size but is restricted to music from MIDI instruments.

▷ Sound compression programs use repetition, averaging, selectivity, and range reduction to reduce file size as much as possible while maintaining as much quality as possible.

▷ Sound-editing software lets you capture, edit, combine, compress, and save sound files for use in a Web site.

▷ You can embed sounds in your Web page or link sounds from a Web page to open in a separate window.

☆ Online References

Sources for MIDI files
Ifni MIDI music `http://www.ifnimidi.com/`
MusicNet `http://musicnetmusic.free.fr/musicnetmusic2.html`

Sources for sound-editing software
Macromedia SoundEdit `http://www.macromedia.com/software/sound/`
Syntrillium CoolEdit Pro and CoolEdit 2000 `http://www.cooledit.com/`
SonicFoundry SoundForge `http://www.sonicfoundry.com/products/`
Macromedia Flash `http://www.macromedia.com/software/flash/`

Sources for sampled music
Free Music Directory `http://www.angelgrrl.com/directory/`

Sources for streaming server software
Information on RealVideo server and RealProducer software `http://www.realnetworks.com`
Information on QuickTime Streaming server and QuickTime Player Pro `http://quicktime.apple.com`
Information on Windows Media applications `http://www.microsoft.com`

☆ Review Questions

1. List some of the possibilities for communication that are offered by using sound on a Web page. Also list some pitfalls and warnings about the use of sound.

2. Explain the difference between sampled sound and MIDI sound.

3. Describe how sampled sound works in a computer.

4. Explain at least two techniques used by codecs to compress sound data.

5. Explain the differences between downloaded sound and streaming sound on a Web page.

6. List the hardware and software you need to capture and edit sound for use on a Web site.

7. List the steps in preparing sound for use on a Web site.

8. Explain the differences between embedded and linked sound on a Web page.

☆ Hands-On Exercises

1. Find three examples on the Web where sound is used as an integral part of the site's purposes. For each one, determine the following:
   (a) Whether the sound is voice, music, or sound effects
   (b) Whether the sound captures attention, explains a process, provides a personal contact, or sets a mood
   (c) Whether it is downloaded or streamed
   (d) The plug-in used to play the sound
   (e) The size of the sound file (for downloaded sound only)
   (f) How long it took for the sound to arrive

2. Capture voice from a live source. Edit it as necessary, and save it in a format suitable for use on a Web page.

3. Convert music from a CD into an editable form, and save it in a format suitable for a Web page.

4. Compress each of the sounds created in Exercises 2 and 3 with different methods, to result in low- and high-quality sound files. Note the file size of each.

5. For each of the sounds created in Exercises 2 and 3, create a Web page that embeds the sound, and another that links to the sound. For the embedded sound, play it on a Web page with a controller that doesn't play until the user clicks but that loops the sound after it's been played once.

CHAPTER FIVE

VIDEO ON THE WEB

Video is the most complex of the multimedia technologies used on the Web. This chapter explores the ways that video can be used on a Web site and explains how video works and the methods used to compress it. You'll also learn how to prepare video for the Web and how to embed video on a Web page.

Chapter Objectives

- To become aware of the possibilities for using video to help accomplish the goals of your Web site
- To understand how video works on the Web, including digitization, compression, and streaming
- To learn how to prepare video for use on a Web site, including shooting, digitizing, editing, and compressing
- To find out how to include video on a Web page by embedding or linking

◎◎ The Possibilities of Video on the Web

Although video is new to the World Wide Web, its origins go all the way back to the ancient Greeks, who rendered important stories by combining the human voice with the gestures of actors, presenting the works in huge outdoor arenas. This combination of communication forms worked well. Audiences loved Greek drama because the combination of forms and the clever storytellers' techniques evoked powerful responses among the audience. This dramatic tradition in the Western world continued down through Shakespeare, Ibsen, and other masters of the dramatic arts.

Drama is a multimedia experience because it combines more than one form of communication. And because the story is presented over time through the movement of the characters, drama adds another dimension to the communication: animation. Drama is the mother of film and video.

The History of Video

Film was the first technology to capture the full multimedia experience of drama and save it in a form that could be distributed widely and extend over time. Invented at the beginning of the twentieth century, film developed as an independent art form with its own industry. Fifty years later, television arrived. It offered a way to capture the combined media of voice, image, gesture, music, and motion just as film did, but distributed by electronic signals rather than film. Today, television and movies are broadcast as well as saved and distributed on videotape and digital videodiscs (DVDs). As increasing numbers of movies are shot and edited in purely digital form, without the use of film at all, the distinction between film and video is blurring.

What video offers is a compelling experience that can include images, voice, music, and motion. Video can be all-consuming, monopolizing our eyes as well as our ears, providing something new to see and hear every moment. Because of this, video is the most popular form of mass communication in the United States; we spend more time with this medium than with all the others combined.

It's no wonder that people are beginning to include video on their Web sites. Even though most of the Web audience lacks the bandwidth to enjoy high-quality video, things are changing quickly. Increasing numbers of offices and schools have installed high-speed networks that make video possible, and DSL and cable modems, which can transmit medium-quality video, are becoming more widely installed in homes. At the same time, the technologies for compressing video are moving forward, allowing us to get more quality from the same bandwidth.

Some people say that the television and the computer will merge in the near future—we'll watch TV on our computers and use our TV sets to browse the Web. Whether or not this prediction proves true, the inescapable trend is toward a convergence of the most popular medium (video) and the fastest-growing medium (the computer connected to the Internet).

The first step along this path—a step you can take today—is the inclusion of video material in your Web site.

The Role of Video on a Web Site

Video changes the way visitors experience a Web page. Video can do things that are impossible with text and still images and sound, and in a manner that's hard to ignore. Video can tell a story, entertain an audience, explain a complex process, and bring a personal touch to the communication.

Telling a Story

It might be a news anchor breaking the story of a revolution in Africa, complete with live coverage from the capital and interviews with experts. It might be a professor of literature recounting an author's narrative over shots of the locations described in the book. It might be a scene from *Romeo and Juliet*, in which viewers witness the feud between the Montagues and the Capulets. For centuries, we have been sharing news as well as classic stories, and we are drawn to this form of communication like no other. Storytelling may be video's greatest strength on the Web.

☆ **DO IT YOURSELF**   **View Web Video News**

Visit the sites of the major news organizations on the Web: ABC News, CNN, FoxNews, and the others. Study how they use video to tell stories. Notice how many stories are available and how they change every day. Notice also that news sites don't use video alone, as on television. Rather, they use video combined and linked a wealth of additional information in many different forms.

☆ **DO IT YOURSELF**   **View Web Movies**

Visit the sites of movie producers, and watch some of their trailers. Try Paramount Pictures (`http://www.paramount.com/`), Sony Pictures (`http://www.sonypictures.com/`), or iFilm (`http://www.ifilm.com/`). Or see trailers from many different producers at the QuickTime movie trailers page (`http://www.apple.com/trailers/`). You will find many kinds and forms of storytelling on these sites, with some of the best video quality on the Web.

☆ **DO IT YOURSELF**   **Watch Web Video Stories**

Visit the Web site of WGBH (`http://broadband.wgbh.org/`) and watch one of its "netcasts." You'll find many kinds of stories being told through the video medium.

☆ **TIP**   **Limitations of Video**

As you visit video-rich sites, you'll experience the two limitations of video on the Web: bandwidth bottleneck and plug-in perplexity. Depending on the speed of your connection, you may find the highest-quality video difficult to watch. Also, you may have to download and install various plug-ins. It's a good idea to keep track of your experience. It will help you plan the best way to serve the needs of your own site's audience.

Does your Web site have any stories to tell? Can video help get those stories across effectively? Later in this chapter, you'll learn how to develop a video that can tell a story on your site.

Entertaining Viewers

Most of what we watch on television is entertainment, designed to keep us watching so that we'll be there for the commercials. The craft of designing attention-keeping video has gown to an art form during the past half-century of television. From *Comedy Central* to *Survivor*, from Oprah to the Oscars, we can be alternately amused, excited, shocked, or moved to sympathy by the power of video.

⭐ **DO IT YOURSELF**   **Experience Web Video Entertainment**

To see how entertaining video can be on the Web, visit the BMW Films site (`http://www.bmwfilms.com/`), *The Simpsons* (`http://thesimpsons.com/`), *Comedy Central* (`http://www.comedycentral.com/`) or MTV (`http://www.mtv.com`). Notice that the experience is not the same as television: There's more user choice, more control, more mixing with other media, including animation, images, text, and audio. These Web sites are truly multimedia. They contain videos that have never appeared on television but instead were developed exclusively for the Web.

⭐ **DO IT YOURSELF**   **Think About Your Audience**

Does the audience for your Web site need to be entertained? Might an entertaining video keep them glued to your site? Might a humorous or dramatic video help communicate one of your site's key points?

Explaining a Process

Sometimes video is the best way to explain a scientific process or illustrate a philosophical principle.

⭐ **DO IT YOURSELF**   **Watch Explanatory Web Video**

To see how video is used to explain concepts and processes that would be difficult to show in any of the other media, check out the Great Bear site at Greenpeace (`http://www.greenpeace.org/greatbear/`), *Chemistry TV* at the University of Oxford (`http://www.chem.ox.ac.uk/vrchemistry/chemistrytv/chemistrytv.html`), or *This Old House* (`http://www.pbs.org/wgbh/thisoldhouse/`).

Great Bear explains the geography and ecology of the Northwest coast using dramatic video footage and other media techniques. Molecules and atoms rotate and transform in the chemistry education videos from Oxford (see Figure 5.1). *This Old House* shows time-lapse video of building and restoration techniques in the rebuilding of historic homes. In these examples, and in many others, video on the Web serves a serious educational purpose.

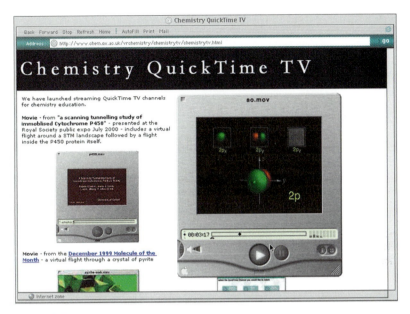

Figure 5.1 Chemistry TV

How might video help explain a concept or process on your Web site?

Personalizing the Web Experience

Visit the Web site of The Callidus Company (`http://www.callidussoftware.com/improvingbusinessperformance.asp`), and watch CEO Reed Taussic tell you about the company on live streaming video, as illustrated in Figure 5.2. Video can give Web visitors a sense of personal connection that can help an organization distinguish itself from its competitors.

Or imagine the hypothetical Web site of Fred's Storm Door Company (introduced in Chapter Four). Picture Fred, in full-motion video, demonstrating one of his famous doors and welcoming you to his company and its site. On your computer screen, Fred becomes a live human personality. His appearance in video makes the site seem alive, dynamic and moving, rather than a collection of static text and pictures.

These kinds of videos need not be long or profound. They simply establish the face, the voice, and the gestures of the person behind the company. How might you establish this kind of personal connection on your site? What content would be effective? Where would it appear?

☆ **DO IT YOURSELF**   **Plan Your Video**

Create a plan for the videos you might use on your Web site. For each video, explain its purpose, content, and location on the site. Also explain the situation of your audience in terms of bandwidth and plug-ins.

Figure 5.2 Personal Video Message from Callidus CEO

◎◎ How Video Works on the Web

Video on the Web works differently from film, TV video, and videotape. It uses different technologies and different storage and transmission methods. Still in its infancy, the Web video industry is undergoing rapid change as new approaches and technologies are invented.

Video on the Web is fully digital, and it must undergo significant compression to be useful. It can be downloaded as a file or streamed to the audience. Its file formats and codecs are complex and competitive.

Digital Video

Traditional video material is analog: It is stored and transmitted in a form that mirrors its natural appearance. A television camera scans the event, converting the light that enters the camera into electrical impulses that match the brightness of the light. The scan proceeds as a set of narrow lines across the image, 525 lines from top to bottom, scanned 30 times each second. A continuous signal is produced and is sent via cables and radio waves to the television receiver, which displays the lines on the screen in the same continuous 525 lines 30 times each second.

Videotape simply stores this continuous stream of analog electrical impulses so that it can be saved and played back to a receiver. Figure 5.3 shows a diagram of this analog system.

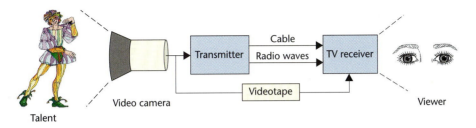

Figure 5.3 The Analog Video System

But as you learned in Chapter Four, a computer is not equipped to receive and store this kind of information in its continuous, analog form. It must digitize the signal, turning it into a series of discrete numbers that can be saved in a file. This system is called **digital video (DV)**. Instead of scanning the event in a continuous stream, the digital video camera takes a snapshot of the event 30 times per second. Each snapshot is recorded by an array of light-sensitive crystals inside the camera, in most cases 700 pixels wide and 525 pixels high.

As with still images, each snapshot, or **frame**, of video is divided into pixels, typically 367,500 of them. The light-sensitive array records the color and brightness of the light received at each pixel as a number, which is saved on the camera's storage medium. Most often, the numbers are stored on a magnetic tape inside the camera, called a **DV cartridge**, as a long series of numbers. Figure 5.4 shows this system.

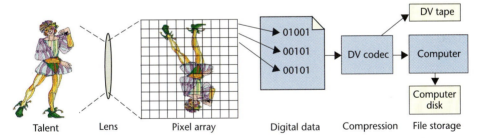

Figure 5.4 The Digital Video System

Think of how many numbers that would be. The camera sends 367,500 numbers per frame, 30 frames per second. Each second of video produces more than 10 million (10,000,000) numbers, at least 10MB per second. So to store all the frames of an episode of *The Simpsons*, for example, would require 19,845MB of numbers. That's too many for most computers and most Internet connections to handle. So the video data is compressed, just as image and sound data is compressed.

The first round of compression takes place in the DV camera: As the numbers are recorded on the DV cartridge, they are compressed using a standard DV compression algorithm. This is accomplished by compression software that's etched on a chip inside the camera. So what ends up on the DV cartridge is a data stream of numbers that represent each frame of the video.

In most cases, this DV data is brought into video-editing software on the computer through an IEEE 1394 connector, often called a **FireWire** connector. Most DV camcorders and most new multimedia computers come equipped with FireWire connectors. Figure 5.5 shows these connectors on a typical camera and computer.

Figure 5.5 FireWire Connectors on a Typical Cable (Left) and Computer

The video-editing software opens a connection to the camcorder, causes the tape inside the DV cartridge to play, and receives the stream of video data. As it comes in, the data is saved to a file on the computer's hard disk, frame by frame.

☆**TIP**   **Analog Video Input**

Analog video data, from an analog camcorder or videotape, can be used in a computer, but it must first be digitized. Analog-to-digital transformation circuitry can reside on a video capture card inside the computer, or inside some DV camcorders. The analog stream of electrical impulses is changed to a frame-by-frame digital data file. This entails some loss of quality and adds an extra step, so it's best to use a DV camcorder and computer with DV input, staying digital all the way.

When these frames are displayed on the computer screen one after another in rapid succession, they give the illusion of continuous motion. In addition, the video file contains a sound track, which contains digital sound data synchronized frame-by-frame to the video. The sound track is digitized by the method described in Chapter Four.

You modify the video using video-editing software, add effects and titles, and then compress and save the final result as a file in a suitable format. (In live streaming video, the file is never saved; rather, the stream of highly compressed video data is packetized and sent over the Internet to the user, whose computer decompresses the data and displays it frame-by-frame on the screen.)

You save the video file in the appropriate directory on your Web server. Then you embed this file into the page or create a link to it. When users open the page or click the link, the video file is downloaded to their hard drive, decompressed by the appropriate plug-in, and displayed on the screen frame-by-frame. (In streaming video, the file is not downloaded to the user's hard drive; rather, it is sent as a string of data from the streaming server to the user's computer, where it is decompressed and displayed frame-by-frame as it arrives.) Figure 5.6 illustrates this sequence.

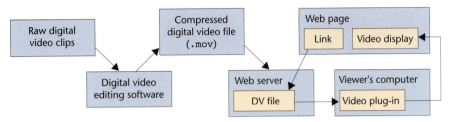

Figure 5.6 Downloading Video on the Web

Compression Methods

Compression is the key to making video work on the Web. Consider the video of *The Simpsons* that you read about: In its uncompressed form, it needs 10MB per second to tell its story. And that's just for the video information; the sound track would add more data! Few if any Internet connections can handle that many megabytes per second. A typical home user with DSL or cable can get perhaps 500 kilobits, or about one-twentieth of a megabyte per second. So to make video work for the Web, it must consume far fewer bits and bytes than in its raw form.

First, the frame size of most video for the Web is reduced. Seldom is video displayed on a Web site at the 700 by 525-pixel size at which it was captured. More typical, as seen in the examples illustrated elsewhere in this chapter, is a 320 by 240-pixel video. This kind of size reduction shrinks the data by more than 75%. That's because a 700 by 525-pixel frame contains 367,500 pixels, whereas the 320 by 240-pixel frame contains only 76,800 pixels.

Next, a video codec is applied to the data in the file. The codec applies as many of the techniques of compression described in Chapter One as will result in less data and reasonable video quality. At the same time, compression is also applied to the sound track, as described in Chapter Three. The following are among the compression techniques that the codec might use.

Repetition and Patterns

Many video files contain a lot of repetition. In frame after frame we see the same blue sky arch over the hero on horseback. The movement of the horse's legs is the same step after step. The codec recognizes this repetition of a single pixel of the same color in a given frame (the clear blue sky) or of a string of numbers over several frames that form a repeated pattern (the horse's moving legs). The codec saves this data using a "ditto, 319 more times," or using a single-number token to represent a repeated pattern. This is the same method used in sound compression codecs. Instead of working with the visual information itself, this method works with the numbers in the video data file. It's all done with math, not with eyes.

This technique of compression is relatively lossless. This means that the decompressor can restore the original data number-by-number, pixel-by-pixel, and frame-by-frame so that the video looks exactly the same as the original. But it's only one approach among many. A good codec combines this technique with the others listed next.

Averaging

Just as the JPEG technique looks at blocks of pixels in a still image and averages their color and brightness, saving one number instead of four or nine or sixteen, so too does a video codec apply averaging to each frame of video. Chapters One and Two describe how this averaging works. In video, each frame is treated as a still image, so it's done 30 times each second. Done selectively, averaging can reduce the amount of data in the file significantly, but it always causes some loss in quality. Done well, the loss in quality is acceptable to the viewer.

Range Reduction

The range in brightness of the original video might be on a scale of 1 to 500, meaning that the lightest part of the sky is 500 times brighter than the darkest shadow under the forest. This brightness information is recorded as a number for each pixel in each frame of the video. This wide range of brightness requires that a big number—8 or 16 bits—be recorded for each pixel. The codec reduces the range to a scale of, say, 1 to 100. The sky is still brighter, but only 100 times or so brighter, and the brightness number can be smaller. Because this number is saved millions of times in the data file, reducing its size can delete lots of data from the file. Most people will not notice this range reduction unless they see the original video and the range-reduced video side-by-side.

Frame-Difference

Picture a baseball game on television. You're seeing the ballpark from the camera in center field. Frame by frame, the video is displayed on the screen. The pitcher winds up, the flag waves—but most of the picture does not move at all. The fielders crouch. The batter maintains his stance. The grass, the dirt basepaths, the scoreboard, the foul lines, all remain exactly the same, frame after frame. The grass alone accounts for most of the pixels in each frame. Is it really necessary to send all those unchanging green pixels in every frame?

For Web viewers to enjoy the game, all we need to send are the pixels that change: the pitcher's motion as he winds up, the batter running down the first base line, the fielder scooping up the grounder. But these changes are small, representing perhaps 5% of the pixels on the screen. The rest of the pixels do not change from frame to frame. A good video codec applies a frame-difference algorithm to save data by recording only the pixels that change from frame to frame.

For the first frame of the video, every pixel is recorded. But for the second frame, only those pixels that change are recorded; the rest is "ditto." This process continues throughout the video. To ensure that what the viewer sees remains true to the original, most codecs send a keyframe—data on every pixel—every 100 frames or so. For video such as a baseball game, where much of the picture is static, this frame-difference technique results in an enormous reduction in the amount of data. But for video with lots of full-screen movement, especially pans and zooms, this approach is not as effective. Thus, the amount of compression varies with the nature of the video material.

Most video codecs apply several of these techniques to reduce file size while maintaining video quality. The result of all this compression is a video file that is small enough to make it through the bandwidth bottleneck quickly enough to let viewers see the video in a reasonable amount of time.

As a Web developer, you don't need to master the arcane arts and statistical sciences behind these video compression techniques. Your video-editing software usually applies the codecs automatically. In some cases, though, you may get to choose which codec to use or how much compression to apply, and you'll learn about these choices later in this chapter.

Downloading versus Streaming

Video on the Web can come to the viewer in three ways: by downloading, by fast-start downloading, or by streaming.

Downloading

This is the simplest method. When the user receives the Web page containing a video, the video file is downloaded from the Web server to the hard drive on the viewer's computer. When the download is complete, the video begins playing. This is the same method used to display images. It's easy to set up, requires no special server, and works with all browsers and all types of connections. But it can take a long time for the file to complete downloading. On a 56K modem, it would take a typical 5MB video file more than 15 minutes to download—too long a wait for most viewers.

After the video is downloaded to the user's hard disk, it remains available and can be saved, used again, copied to a CD, or sent across the local area network. This can be an advantage in some situations but a drawback in others; some owners of video material do not want their products copied by users. For their part, many users will not have room on their disks to store such large files. So this method is best used for small video files of less than a few megabytes, where copying is not an issue.

Fast-Start Downloading

In this method, the video file downloads to the viewer's computer but begins playing as soon as the first few hundred frames have been received. The downloading continues as the video plays. In the end, the downloaded file sits on the viewer's disk, just as in the first method, but there is not as long a wait to see the video.

This method works well for small and medium-size videos through connections that are fast enough to download the data faster than it's needed for playback. Fast-start files can be saved and copied. Later in this chapter, you'll learn how to prepare a video file for fast-start downloading.

Neither the download nor the fast-start method requires a special video streaming server. The video files simply reside in a directory on the Web server.

Streaming

A streaming video is displayed on the screen as soon as it arrives on the user's computer. It is not downloaded to the hard disk. A streaming video server manages the connection with the user, monitoring the reception to ensure that the video is arriving fast enough to provide good viewing. After a few seconds of **data buffering** (temporarily storing portions of the data), the video appears on the user's computer and continues playing as long as the connection is maintained with the streaming server.

Streaming has several advantages. It can present very long (and large) videos that would be much too big to fit on most users' hard disks. It can present live video, in real time, something that's impossible through the download methods. And it can preserve the security of the video files because they never reside on the user's hard disk. But streaming requires a video-streaming server along with significant bandwidth from the server to handle multiple streams. And because it often uses the Real Time Streaming Protocol (RTSP), instead of the more common Hypertext Transport Protocol (HTTP), it can face difficulty in getting past some Internet firewalls.

For streaming video to work for the audience, its data rate must be less than the user's bandwidth. The **data rate** is the amount of video data that's sent in the stream each second; it is determined by the techniques and codecs used to compress the streaming video. A typical data rate for a good-quality 320 by 240-pixel streaming video with sound would be 200 kilobits per second. This would be too many data for a 56K modem, but it's well within the capabilities of most DSL or cable connections, which are often about 500 kilobits.

To originate live streaming video, the codec must work very quickly, compressing the data in real time as it arrives from the camera and then packetizing it and sending it on its way. An encoder computer receives the video data, digitizes it if necessary, and, in most cases, compresses it using a codec designed for live streams. Then the encoder computer packetizes the data from the live stream and sends the packets to a streaming video server. All this happens in real time. The streaming video server then distributes the streams to the various viewers. Figure 5.7 shows this system.

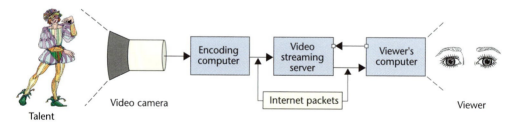

Figure 5.7 Live Streaming Video Setup

The data rate is critical here. The live **Webcast** producer must adjust the encoding software so as to achieve a data rate that's low enough to get through the bandwidth bottleneck of the typical audience, but high enough to ensure viewing quality. In fact, many of the encoding programs, such as Sorenson Broadcaster, provide a real-time monitor that displays the data rate of the outgoing stream.

The three most popular streaming systems are RealVideo, QuickTime, and Windows Media Player. Each provides its own proprietary encoding and streaming software along with a freely downloadable plug-in that enables users to decompress and display the video stream.

> ⭐ **DO IT YOURSELF**   **Which Kind of Video?**
>
> Determine which type of video—downloaded or streaming—is best for your Web site. Also find out what kind of video streaming server is available at your organization.

File Formats for Video

For video files that will be downloaded, the most popular formats for the Web today are as follows.

⭐ QuickTime (`.mov`) was developed by Apple Computer but can be played and used for authoring on all platforms. The QuickTime Player and Plug-in can display video in a variety of other file formats, including `.avi` and `.mpg`, and can handle a variety of codecs for audio and video.

⭐ Moving Picture Experts Group (`.mpg`) is an ISO standards group that devised the MPEG system of compressing video and animation data files. Both QuickTime and Windows Media Player can display `.mpg` files.

⭐ Audio-Video Interleaved (`.avi`) was developed by Microsoft and Intel as a format to store and display video files with sound. You can play `.avi` files using the Windows Media or QuickTime plug-in.

The QuickTime and AVI file formats define the way the data is stored in the file. These formats can use a variety of codecs to compress the data. MPEG defines the compression scheme as well as the file format.

For streaming video, the three most popular file formats are as follows.

⭐ RealVideo (`.ram`) was developed by RealNetworks to work with the RealVideo server and RealVideo plug-in.

⭐ QuickTime (`.mov`) was developed by Apple Computer and designed to work with the QuickTime streaming server, the QuickTime plug-in, and the QuickTime Player.

⭐ Windows Media (`.asf`) was developed by Microsoft to work with the Windows Media Server and the Windows Media Player plug-in.

RealVideo and Windows Media use their own single proprietary codecs; the QuickTime format can use a variety of codecs for compression and decompression.

The file format you choose depends on its compatibility with your video-editing software, the plug-ins your audience is likely to have, and the streaming server your organization uses.

Preparing Video for the Web

To prepare a video for use on a Web site, you first obtain the video content, either by shooting it with a camcorder or copying it from a videotape, laserdisc, CD-ROM, or DVD. Then you get the video data into your computer. If it's in analog form, you must digitize it; if it's in digital form, you can simply copy it. Then you edit the video, combining clips and adding narration, titles, transitions, and other effects. Next, you compress and save the edited video in a suitable file format. Finally, you copy the video file to the appropriate Web server or video-streaming server. For standard Web video, the steps in this process are no different from those for preparing images or sound.

The process is a bit different for originating a live streaming video Webcast, as described later in this chapter.

Sources for Video

The video can come from a variety of sources, such as existing clips or video you shoot. Here's how to use each source.

Camcorder

You use a camcorder to shoot your own video or to play back prerecorded video. Camcorders come in two flavors: analog and digital. Newer digital (DV) camcorders send their data to the computer via a FireWire (IEEE 1394) cable. Older analog camcorders send their data over RCA cables and require that the computer be equipped with a video-digitizing board.

> ⭐ **SHORTCUT**   You'll find tips on shooting original video later in this chapter.

Videotape

Standard VHS videocassette tape stores the video in analog form, and the output from the VHS VCR is also analog video. To get your video from this source, your computer must be equipped with a video-digitizing card. The audio and video outputs of the VCR are connected to the audio and video inputs of the computer's digitizing circuitry with standard RCA cables.

> ⭐ **TIP**   **Video Digitizing versus Digital Video**
>
> Most computers aren't equipped with circuitry to digitize analog video. A few older models of the Apple Macintosh, called AV models, include the circuitry, but on virtually all Windows computers video digitizing is an expensive extra. Modern Macintosh computers come equipped with the FireWire connector for digital video, and the standardized FireWire can be added to a Windows computer for a reasonable cost.

Laserdisc

A laserdisc player can be connected to a computer in the same way as a VHS VCR. Because the output from the laserdisc player is analog, you will need video-digitizing circuitry in the computer to use this source.

DVD

Although the video on a DVD itself is in digital form, the output of a DVD player is standard analog video. Thus, you connect a DVD player to the computer in the same way that you connect a VCR or laserdisc, and it requires digitizing circuitry. There is no easy way to get the digital video files from a commercial DVD directly into your computer.

Television

If your television set or tunable VCR has audio and video outputs, you can bring live television into your video-editing software by connecting these outputs to the video digitizer in your computer via standard RCA cables (see Figure 5.8). This works in the same way as the VCR.

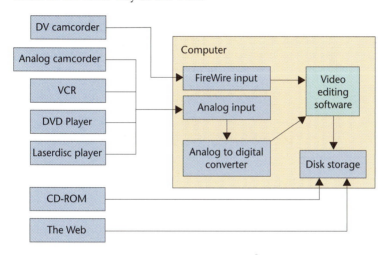

Figure 5.8 Connecting Video Sources to the Computer

> ⭐ **WARNING** **Whose Video Is It?**
>
> Unless you shot the video yourself, you cannot use it on your Web site without permission from its owner. Most video on VHS tapes, television, DVD, and laserdisc belongs to someone else, and you must get permission to include it on a public Web site.

CD-ROM

Video files on a CD-ROM are already in digital form, and the files are usually in `.mov`, `.avi`, or `.mpg` format. To be used on a Web site, they need only be copied from the CD to your hard disk, or opened in an application such as QuickTime Player Pro and then saved to your disk.

Web Video

Web video that you download to your computer can usually be saved and used on your own site, providing you have permission from the owner. The best way to capture this video is to set QuickTime as your helper application for `.mov`, `.mpg`, and `.avi` video (to do this, go to the Preferences section of your browser); then you save the video as soon as it completes its download. But streaming video, such as RealPlayer video, cannot be used because it never downloads to your hard drive. Many publishers use streaming video for this reason.

Video from Still Images

Ken Burns's documentary on the Civil War contains no video material from the war itself or of the people or countryside of mid-nineteenth-century America—neither video nor film had been invented in 1860. Instead, Burns used photographs and paintings from the era. He combined these still images, panning and zooming them, adding transitions, music, and a narrative, into a high-quality video experience.

You can do the same, building a video from a series of still images. The images must be of good quality and saved at 700 by 525 pixels (the size of the video-editing screen) in JPEG format. To fill the screen properly, the images must be at this size and must have a 4:3 **aspect ratio**. Accompanying music should be saved in `.aif` or other format compatible with your video-editing software. Narration can be recorded live in the video editor or saved in `.aif` format.

> ⭐ **TIP   Aspect Ratio**
>
> Standard video that we see on television is wider than it is tall. In fact, it's exactly four units wide and three units high. The ratio of height to width of a video (or of an image) is called its aspect ratio.

Using a Video Camera to Shoot Video

Shooting your own video guarantees that you are its owner, and it lets you customize the material. Whether you shoot live, connecting the camera to the computer and bringing the video directly into the editor, or store it on tape or DV cartridge for later transfer to the computer, here are some tips for getting good-quality video.

Know Your Purpose

Why is this video on the Web site? What purpose does it serve? What's the point that you want this scene or this interview to make? Why video—why not do it with text and images? For efficient planning, it's essential to keep your purpose clear and to make everyone in the video aware of the ultimate goal of the shoot.

Use a Tripod

If possible, mount your camera on a tripod. No matter how steady you think you are, the motion of your body and hands will affect the shot and make it harder to view (and to compress). A tripod is neither expensive nor difficult to set up, and all video cameras come with a standard threaded mount to fit the tripod.

Beware the Background

What will be in the background of your shot? A busy street with people moving by? A thick forest of dark green? A plain white wall? A window? Plan your background just as carefully as you plan the elements in the foreground. Placing the **talent** (people appearing on-camera) in front of an appropriate background can lend context and reality to the scene. But a background that's too busy and full of movement can distract viewers and make the clip harder to compress.

Watch the Light

Don't shoot directly into the light or with the light directly behind you. Light should strike the subject from the side and top, creating natural shadows and texture. Use natural light, but don't be afraid to supplement it with a carefully placed light source. Watch for shadows that you create the light source you use. Most video cameras adjust themselves automatically to the light, so look through the viewfinder to see the scene as the camera will record it.

Use an External Microphone

Any video clip that will include sound needs an external microphone. The microphone that's built into the camera is usually too far away from the subject. It will pick up the noises of your hands touching the camera, vibrations from the tripod, the wind, and even the breathing of the camera operator. For interviews, use a microphone that clips onto the collar of the speaker. All video cameras come equipped with a connector for an external microphone.

Zoom In for a Close Shot

Video on the Web is smaller than video on television. In most cases, your subject will never appear more than 320 pixels wide and 240 pixels high. So it's important to make your subject fill what little space there is in the video window. Let your subject fill the screen, even bleed over the edges a bit. Avoid long shots and large group scenes—the details will not be visible on the Web. Whatever level of detail you see in the viewfinder, count on about half that resolution on the final Web video.

Use DV

If at all possible, use a digital video camera and DV input to the computer. This avoids the analog-to-digital conversion that reduces quality and takes time.

Shoot Several Takes

⭐ **SHORTCUT**   Staying digital all the way—from the shooting to the storage to the transfer to the editing to the saving of the final file—results in a more efficient process, less work, and a much higher quality product.

Shoot the scene or the interview more than once, simply repeating the process. This gives you more than one clip to choose from as you compile the video in the editor, and it insures against unnoticed glitches and mistakes.

Shoot Some B-roll

While you're on location with the camera, take some footage of adjacent scenes or subject matter that an interviewee refers to. These clips can later be interspersed with the main video to provide an interesting storytelling technique.

⭐ **DO IT YOURSELF**   Shoot Some Video

Following the guidelines here, shoot some original video for your Web site.

> ★ **TIP**   **Video Vocabulary**
>
> Many of the terms associated with making video for the Web come from the traditions of film and television. **Footage** refers to the number of feet of film that snake through the camera as a shot is filmed. **B-roll** refers to the film or videotape that was set rolling on reel B while the main video was rolling on reel A; in this way, when the time comes to add the secondary material, it's ready to go. The concept of **shooting** came from film, as did the idea of **takes** (shooting a scene more than once). **Scene** comes from ancient drama.

Digitizing and Storing Video

Now that you have your video clips, it's time to get the video material into your computer so that you can edit it. The video must be in digital form and in a compatible file format.

Analog Video

If your source is analog video—such as a VHS tape or output from a DVD, laserdisc player, or analog camcorder—you must digitize it in one of two ways:

 If your computer has analog-to-digital video circuitry, usually evident as a set of RCA connectors labeled *video input*, you connect the source (camcorder, VHS VCR, laserdisc player, or DVD) outputs to the computer's video inputs, as shown in Figure 5.8. Then launch the **video capture** feature of your editing software, play the source, and watch it on the computer screen. Click Record to start capturing the video (and audio, in most cases). Click Stop to end the capture. Enter a filename for this clip and save it in `.avi` or `.mov` format.

 If your computer has a FireWire (DV) connector, you use a special converter or a DV camcorder to transform the analog video signal to a digital form that can travel through the FireWire. Connect the source (camcorder, VHS VCR, laserdisc player, or DVD) outputs to the DV camcorder's analog connector. Connect the FireWire cable from the DV camcorder to the computer. Launch the DV editing software. Set the DV camcorder's mode, if necessary, to *A/V in*. Set the source to play. You should see the video in the editor's input window. Click Capture or Import to start the capture, and Stop to end it. The clip will be saved in DV format.

Digital Video

Working with digital video is much easier. Simply connect the FireWire cable from the DV camcorder to the computer. Launch the DV editing software on the computer. In the editing window, click Play to start the DV cartridge rolling, and you'll see the video in the window. Click Capture or Import to start the capture, and Stop to end it. The clips are automatically saved in DV format on the hard disk.

Don't Capture Everything

You need not digitize the entire reel. Not all the clips you took will be needed in the final video, so capture and store only those pieces of video that you're sure you will use. Capturing takes time and disk space, so digitize only what's necessary. You should capture a few seconds before and after the clips so that you can trim them properly in the editor (discussed later in this chapter). But it makes little sense to capture the outtakes.

Software Tools for Editing Video

Now it's time to edit and assemble the final product. Which editor is best? For digital video editing, there are three levels of products:

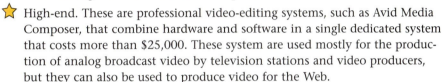 High-end. These are professional video-editing systems, such as Avid Media Composer, that combine hardware and software in a single dedicated system that costs more than $25,000. These system are used mostly for the production of analog broadcast video by television stations and video producers, but they can also be used to produce video for the Web.

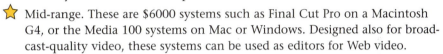 Mid-range. These are $6000 systems such as Final Cut Pro on a Macintosh G4, or the Media 100 systems on Mac or Windows. Designed also for broadcast-quality video, these systems can be used as editors for Web video.

Consumer level. Designed for home and semiprofessional video production, these include Adobe Premiere and EditDV on both Mac and Windows, and iMovie on Macintosh. EditDV and iMovie are designed exclusively for digital video and are easier to use in this mode. Such systems cost about $1500.

The consumer-level systems are more than adequate for the production of video for the Web. Any advantages of the high-end systems are lost when the file is reduced in size and quality for use on the Web. Remember that for most audiences, full-screen video cannot be included on a Web page. The examples in this book use Premiere and iMovie, the most popular consumer-level video editors.

No matter which tool you choose, the process of editing video is the same. It follows these steps:

1. Draw a storyboard.

2. Capture the clips in the editor.

3. Import the other media elements, such as still images.

4. Trim the clips to the right length.

5. Arrange the clips and other elements along a timeline.

6. Add titles and transitions.

7. Add audio narration and music.

8. Save the completed video in the proper format for the Web, compressing it in the process.

Along the way, you'll do lots of previewing and revising of your work. Producing a video is more art than science, so you'll find plenty of opportunity for second thoughts and revisions. The editors are designed to make this easy.

Storyboarding

Before you start, it's a good idea to draw a **storyboard** for your video. This planning diagram shows what comes first, second, and so on. It includes visual elements as well as sound, titles, and narration. Figure 5.9 shows a storyboard for a typical Web video.

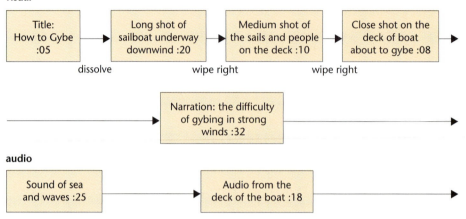

Figure 5.9 Part of a Storyboard for a Web Video

Each box shows a **visual element**, which might be a video clip, a still picture, or a title. Along the bottom are the **sound tracks**, including narration, sound from the video clip, music, or sound effects. Between the clips, the storyboard shows any **transitions** that you plan to use. It also shows the estimated **timing** for each section of the video.

To complete your storyboard, you may need to look again at your video clips, write the copy for any narration, and locate any music or sound effects that you need.

☆**WARNING** Whose Music Is It?

Most music that you hear on the radio or get from CDs belongs to its composer and performer. Without their permission, you cannot include the music as part of a Web video. For a class project that's shared only between you and your teacher, such use may not be illegal, but you should be aware of the copyright that applies to music.

Before they edit the material, many Web developers send the storyboard to the editor or other organizational official responsible for the content of the site. Most professional video editors print a copy of the storyboard and keep it in front of them throughout the editing.

☆**DO IT YOURSELF**   Draw a Storyboard

Use pencil and paper, or the drawing tools in Microsoft Word, to create a storyboard for your video. Include visual elements, audio, timing, titles, and transitions, as shown in the example.

Capturing the Clips

You may already have done this in the process of digitizing and storing your video. Otherwise, now's the time. The captured clips will appear in a window in the editor; in iMovie it's called the **shelf**, and in Premiere it's called the **clips window**. Each clip is represented by a single frame of the video. Figure 5.10 shows several clips on the shelf in iMovie.

Figure 5.10 Video Clips on the Shelf in iMovie

For now, leave the clips where they are; later you'll trim them and drag them into the timeline.

Importing the Other Media Elements

Few videos consist solely of video clips. Many contain still images, titles, music, narration, and other media elements. No matter which editor you are using, now's the time to import any still images that you will need. Click Import from the File menu and find the image file you need; it will appear in the shelf or the clips window. If you want the still image to fill the screen, it should be 640 pixels wide and 480 pixels high (for a DV editor such as iMovie), or the exact size of the video window if you're using Premiere.

If you're using Premiere, you should also import the narration, titles, and music now. If you're using iMovie, you can bring them directly into the timeline as you need them.

Trimming the Clips

Each of your video clips must be trimmed so that it starts and stops on the proper frame. Select the video in the clips area, and it will display in the window shown in Figure 5.11.

Figure 5.11 Trimming a Clip in the Editing Window

Here are the remaining steps in trimming the clips:

 With Premiere, use the controller to display the frame where you want the clip to start. This is called the **in** point. Click the button to set this as the in point. Do the same for the ending frame, or **out** point.

 With iMovie, hold down [Shift] and drag the **scrubber bar**, as shown in Figure 5.11, to select the frames you want to cut. You will probably need to cut some from the beginning of the clip as well as some from the end. You can also use this method to cut frames from the middle of the clip.

Trim all your video clips in this manner until they include exactly the video you want to appear in the final product.

☆**WARNING** **Don't Trim Too Close**

When you're trimming frames, save room for any transitions you plan to use. For a quick transition, leave about a second of video before and after. For a slow transition, leave about two seconds. That's because a transition combines some frames from one clip with some frames from the next; a one-second transition requires 30 frames from each clip. During these transition frames, the video is not fully visible because its pixels are combined with the pixels from the preceding clip.

☆**DO IT YOURSELF**   **Add Media Elements and Trim the Clips**

Use the editor to capture and trim your video clips. Also import still images and other media into the editor.

Arranging Visuals along the Timeline

Now comes the assembly of the elements of the video. For still images and video clips, simply drag the item from the clip window or shelf into the visual portion of the timeline, as shown in Figure 5.12. They should be arranged one after another in the order that they are shown in the storyboard.

Figure 5.12 Video Clips and Still Images in the iMovie Timeline

Video clips will appear for the length of time to which they were trimmed. To set the length of time that still images will appear, type the number of seconds in the appropriate box, as shown in Figure 5.12.

Adding Titles

Titles are simply visual elements. They can appear by themselves over black or another solid color, or they can appear over video clips or still images, as shown in Figure 5.13.

Figure 5.13 Two Kinds of Titles

First, determine the words of the title. Then follow these steps:

⭐ In Premiere, you created title files earlier in the process. The title files should be imported into the Clips window. Now drag the title from the clip window into the S, or **superimpose**, track of the timeline. To make the title display on top of an existing video clip or still image, set its background to `transparent` using the Title item in the File menu.

⭐ In iMovie, choose the Title tab (see Figure 5.14), and then type the title into the fields provided. Choose the desired title type from the list. You will see a preview of the title in the little window in the upper left. To show the title by itself, over black, click the Over Black box. To set the length (duration) and speed (how quickly it appears) of the title, drag the sliders under the preview window. When you're happy with the title, drag its T icon to the appropriate place in the timeline.

Figure 5.14 Creating Titles with iMovie

Adding Transitions

Transitions include dissolves, wipes, and other effects that blend the end of one clip with the beginning of the next.

To create a transition with Premiere, you drag one clip to video track A and the next clip to video track B, and then you drag the clips so that they overlap for the desired length of the transition (see Figure 5.15).

In iMovie, simply arrange the clips next to each other, and then click the Transitions tab. Set the length of the transition using the sliders under the preview window. Choose the type of transition from the list, as shown in Figure 5.16. Watch a small preview as you choose. Remember that the transition must be shorter in duration than the clips on either side of it. When you're happy with the preview, drag the transition's T icon into the timeline and drop it between the appropriate clips.

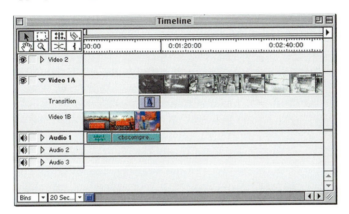

Figure 5.15 Overlapping Video Clips in Premiere

Figure 5.16 Creating Transitions with iMovie

Now that titles and transitions are set, it's a good idea to play the video as a **rough-cut**. Play it several times, and observe the visual effects. Revise the arrangement and transitions as necessary before proceeding to the next steps.

Adding Sound Elements

Sounds go in next: narration, music, and sound effects. These go into their own sound tracks and are combined with the sound tracks from the video clips.

In Premiere, drag the sound from the clips window into one of the open sound tracks, and place it at the appropriate point in the timeline.

In iMovie, click the Sound tab, and use the various tools to record a narration, add sound effects, or add music from a CD (see Figure 5.17). Here's how.

1. To record a narration, place the playhead in the timeline at the point where you want the narration to begin. Speak into the microphone to test the level; it should go into the yellow but not into the red. When you're ready, click the Record Voice button, and speak as you watch the video play. Click Stop when you're finished. You'll see the narration as a colored stripe in one of the audio tracks.

2. To add music from a CD, put the CD into the computer's CD drive. Its list of tracks will appear in the Sound window. Choose a track, clicking the Play button if you want to preview it. Place the playhead in the timeline at the point where you want the music to begin. Click the Record Music button, and watch the music track proceed in the timeline as the video plays. Click Stop to end the music.

3. To add a sound effect, drag one from the list at the top of the Sound window into one of the audio tracks in the timeline, and drop it at the appropriate point.

Figure 5.17 Adding Sound with iMovie

Preparing Video for the Web

To fade a sound in or out, you drag the "rubber bands" in Premiere's sound track, or the Fade In and Fade Out check boxes in iMovie. To adjust the overall level of a sound, use the rubber bands in Premiere, and the sound slider in iMovie.

With the sounds added, it's a good time to play your video in its entirety and to revise it as necessary using the editor.

⭐ **DO IT YOURSELF**   **Add Titles, Transitions, and Sound**

Following the instructions here, add titles, transitions, and sound to your Web video project. Preview it along the way and revise as necessary.

Saving and Compressing

When you're pleased with the results, you can save the movie in proper format for the Web. As you save, you will also compress it.

In Premiere, choose Export from the File menu, and set the items in the dialog boxes to fit the size and file format you have chosen.

In iMovie, click Export from the File menu, and choose QuickTime from the list in the pop-up menu. Then choose the type of file to export.

Here are some suggestions for selecting the parameters of your exported video file.

⭐ *File Format*: Choose QuickTime (`.mov`) or AVI if the video is to be downloaded to the audience. For QuickTime videos, choose Prepare for Internet Streaming, Fast Start from the export options. If it is to be streamed with RealVideo, save it in `.avi` or `.mov` format for now; later you will open it with RealProducer and save it in the RealVideo streaming format. If it is to be streamed with Windows Media, save it now in `.avi` format and open it later with Windows Media Encoder to prepare it for streaming. If it is to be streamed with the QuickTime streaming server, save it in the QuickTime (`.mov`) format.

⭐ *Size*: For Web video, the largest size you can use with most audiences is 320 by 240 pixels. For people with a DSL or cable connection, a file of this size can play as a stream or download in a reasonable time. But if most of your visitors will use a 56K modem, you should choose a smaller size, such as 240 by 180 pixels. If you know that all your visitors enjoy high-speed LAN connections, you might consider specifying 400 by 300 pixels.

⭐ *Frame rate*: As you save the file, the editor will let you choose a frame rate. Most Web video plays at 12 or 15 frames per second, which is fast enough for all except the most motion-intensive material. Choosing a higher frame rate will put the video out of the reach of most of the Web audience.

⭐ *Video codec*: With RealVideo and Windows Media, you have no choice of codec. For QuickTime, the most advanced codec is Sorenson video: It compresses the most with the least loss of quality. If Sorenson is not available, use the Cinepak codec. The Motion JPEG codec in Premiere creates small files but sacrifices considerable quality.

Audio codec: Again, RealVideo and Windows Media give you no choice. With QuickTime, choose the Qualcomm Purevoice codec if the sounds are mostly voice. Use Q-Design Music if it's mostly music.

☆ **DO IT YOURSELF**   **Save and Compress Your Video**

Save and compress your video file in the format that's appropriate to your audience and your server technology.

Preparing Video for Streaming

Streaming video must be saved in a format specific to your streaming video server. The makers of the servers provide special software to help you compress and save the file.

QuickTime Streaming

Open the video file with QuickTime Player Pro, Sorenson Video, or Media Cleaner Pro. Export it to streaming format with a hinted streaming track. For most video, the Sorenson codec gives the best results. Set the data rate to fit your audience: 500K or less for DSL and cable modem users, 50K or less for modem users.

RealVideo Streaming

Open the video file with RealProducer. Follow the instructions for saving in various formats to fit the bandwidth of your audience.

Windows Media Streaming

Open the file with Windows Media Encoder. Follow the instructions for saving in the format that best suits your site's users.

Setting Up Live Streaming

Sometimes you want to Webcast a live streaming video from your site. You can use any of the three streaming video servers mentioned here. To originate a live stream, you need a camcorder, an encoding computer, and a video-streaming server. You also need a robust Internet connection for the encoding computer as well as the server. Table 5.1 shows what's necessary.

Table 5.1 Live Streaming Setup

Source	QuickTime Streaming	RealVideo Streaming	Windows Media Streaming
Camcorder	DV or analog	DV or analog	DV or analog
Encoding computer	Macintosh G3 or better	Macintosh or Windows	Windows2000
Encoding software	Sorenson Broadcaster	RealProducer	Windows Media Encoder

The encoding computer under all three systems must have a FireWire connector or analog-to-digital card to match the type of camcorder that's used. Here are the steps in setting up a live stream from your Web site.

1. Set up the camcorder, microphone, lighting, and talent.

2. In the same location, set up the encoding computer and connect it to the Internet.

3. Launch the encoding software.

4. Ensure that the video and sound from the camcorder are being received by the encoding software.

5. Using the encoding software, set the parameters of the stream: size, frame rate, buffer time, and codecs for video and audio. Also enter the IP address or URL of your video-streaming server. Finally, create a Stream Description Protocol (`.sdp`) file.

6. Copy the `.sdp` file to the proper directory on the video-streaming server. This file serves as a pointer to the incoming stream, describing its parameters.

7. On the encoding computer, begin broadcasting the stream.

8. Go to another computer on the Internet, which you will use as a monitor, and use a browser to connect to the Webcast. (For QuickTime streaming, use QuickTime Player Pro to connect to the Webcast and then to create a reference file with the `.mov` extension.)

9. Embed or link in your Web page the URL of the Webcast (the streaming server's URL plus the video stream filename) or the QuickTime reference file.

Users who connect to your Web page will be able to watch the live streaming video. When the Webcast is over, don't forget to remove the link to the Webcast video, or to change it to connect to an archived copy of the Webcast.

Filenames and Directories for Video on the Web

The filename for a video must be Web-legal, with no spaces or special characters. Best practice also calls for all lowercase letters. The file extension must match exactly the type of the file: `.mov` for a QuickTime video, `.avi` for AVI, `.asf` for Windows Media, and `.ram` for RealVideo. This suffix is usually added automatically as you save the file in the video editor or streaming-preparation software.

Video files that are to be downloaded by users can reside on the Web server along with the image and sound files for the site, and they're often placed in a `media` directory (folder). From there, they are embedded or linked to a Web page.

Video files that are to be streamed must be placed in the proper directory on the video-streaming server. The Web master of the streaming server can tell you exactly where to place these files. Keep careful track of the URL of this location because you will need it to embed or link to these streaming videos.

◎◎ Adding Video to a Web Page

Now you're ready to make your videos a part of your Web site. Like sounds, videos can be embedded so that they display right on the page; or they can be linked to a Web page and display in their own separate window.

Embedding provides a simpler viewer experience and lets you integrate the video more carefully with the other elements on the page. It also lets you set certain user control parameters to control how the video appears on the site.

Linking, on the other hand, sets up a separate display window—typically a window defined by the maker of the streaming server—that users can manipulate independently from the rest of the page content.

Embedding Video with a WYSIWYG Web Page Editor

Embedding a video on a Web page using an editor such as Dreamweaver is very similar to inserting an image or a sound. Follow these steps:

1. Place the pointer at the location where you want the video to appear.

2. From the Insert menu, click Media, and then click Plug-in.

3. In the file section dialog box, choose the video file from the proper directory, or enter its URL. A square with the plug-in icon appears in the document window at the pointer location. This square represents the video.

4. Stretch the square to the length and height of the video, such as 320 pixels wide and 240 pixels high. If you plan to show a controller bar at the bottom, add another 16 pixels to the height of this rectangle.

5. Preview the page in the browser. (The default setting for embedded video is to play as soon as the page loads and to show the controller.)

In the browser, you will see the video with its controller, and the video will play as soon as the page and the file are loaded.

Embedding Video with HTML

To embed a video with HTML, use this code:

```
<embed src="/media/testvideo.mov" width="320"
height="256"></embed>
```

The name of the video file in this example is `testvideo.mov`, and it's in the `media` directory. The video will show 320 pixels wide and 256 pixels high with its controller.

Parameters for Embedded Video

To control the way a video is displayed and controlled by the user, you can set parameters (or attributes) for it. These parameters, which you set when you insert the video, send instructions to the browser and the plug-in about how the video should be shown. In a WYSIWYG editor such as Dreamweaver, you set the parameters by clicking the square plug-in icon, opening its Properties window, and then clicking the Parameters button (see Figure 5.18).

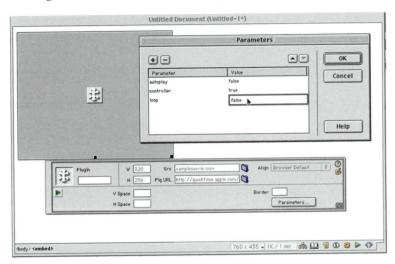

Figure 5.18 Setting Video Parameters in Dreamweaver

Table 5.2 shows some of the parameters.

Table 5.2 Parameters for Controlling Video

Parameter	Values	Result
Autoplay	True or false	Makes the video begin playing as soon as the page is viewed
Controller	True or false	Shows a slider that lets the user stop, start, advance, or rewind the video
Height	Measurement in pixels	Sets the height of the video including its controller
Loop	True or false	Plays the video repeatedly
Width	Measurement in pixels	Sets the width of the video

Here's HTML code for setting parameters for an embedded video:

```
<embed src="/media/testvideo.mov" width="320"
height="240" autoplay="true" controller ="false"
loop="true"></embed>
```

This video would play as soon as it was loaded, show no controller, display at 320 by 240 pixels, and play repeatedly.

☆ **DO IT YOURSELF**   Embed Video

Use a WYSIWYG editor or HTML code to embed a video in a Web page. Test it in both browsers. Then adjust the various parameters and observe how the video behaves.

Linking Video with a WYSIWYG Editor

You can use a linked video when you want your audience to see the video in its own window. You can also use a linked video to let your audience click a button or word on the Web page to bring up the video. Any form of video—downloaded or streaming—can be linked. When the link is clicked, the video opens in its own window.

To link a video from a Web page, follow these steps.

1. Select the item you wish to link from. It can be a word or phrase in the text, a button, an image, or a hot spot in an image map.
2. Click Make Link from the Modify menu.
3. In the file selection box, click the folder icon and then navigate to the video file; or enter its URL.
4. Click OK, and the link is made.
5. Test the link by previewing the page in a Web browser.

The nature of the window that displays the video will depend on the plug-in that's used to play the sound. QuickTime uses a plain window with a simple controller bar. RealPlayer and Windows Media Player open a large window with advertising and progress indicators.

Linking Video with HTML

To link to a video using HTML, use this code:

```
Here is the <a href="/media/testvideo.mov">link</a>.
```

In this example, `link` makes a link to the video file `testvideo.mov` in the `media` directory. Notice that this is the same code that's used to link to any other URL on the Web.

☆ **DO IT YOURSELF**   Link Video

Use a WYSIWYG editor or HTML code to link to a video from a Web page. Test it in both browsers.

Providing User Control

Video offers great possibilities to enhance a Web site and fulfill its purposes. But it also can create difficulties. Think carefully about your audience before including video in your Web site. Consider these questions:

☆ Will your visitors have the bandwidth to play the video? Or might they be better off with a still image accompanied by a voice-over?

⭐ Should the video play automatically as the page opens, uncontrollable by the user? Or should you provide a controller so that the user can stop, start, and repeat the video?

⭐ Should you embed the video into the page and place its controller next to the text or image that accompanies it? Or should you open it in its own window, and risk some confusion as the window opens in front of the Web page and covers its contents?

⭐ On a menu page that users will keep coming back to, is it wise to include a video that plays automatically?

⭐ Will your audience have the patience to wait for your 20MB video file to download? Might you be better off to compress it so that the wait is more reasonable?

When in doubt, it's best to err on the side of user control. Let your audience decide how, when, and where to watch the video. And be courteous—let them turn it off if they'd rather not watch.

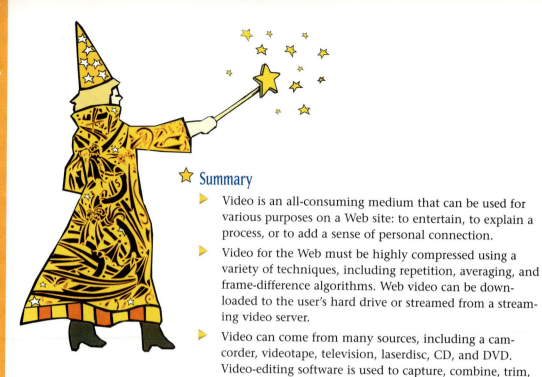

⭐ Summary

▷ Video is an all-consuming medium that can be used for various purposes on a Web site: to entertain, to explain a process, or to add a sense of personal connection.

▷ Video for the Web must be highly compressed using a variety of techniques, including repetition, averaging, and frame-difference algorithms. Web video can be downloaded to the user's hard drive or streamed from a streaming video server.

▷ Video can come from many sources, including a camcorder, videotape, television, laserdisc, CD, and DVD. Video-editing software is used to capture, combine, trim, and edit video with other media elements.

▷ A video can be embedded in a Web page, or it can be linked to a word or image and open in its own window.

⭐ Online References

Information on RealVideo server and RealProducer software
http://www.realnetworks.com

Information on QuickTime streaming server and QuickTime Player Pro
http://quicktime.apple.com

Information on Windows Media applications
http://www.microsoft.com

Information on iMovie
http://iMovie.apple.com

Information on Premiere
http://www.adobe.com

Developing video for the RealVideo server
http://service.real.com/help/library/guides/production/htmfiles/video.htm

⭐ Review Questions

1. List three advantages and two disadvantages of using video on a Web site.

2. Explain the difference between analog and digital video.

3. List at least three techniques used by video compression codecs, and explain how each works to reduce the size of the data file.

4. Explain the difference between streaming and downloaded video.

5. List the hardware and software needed to originate a live streaming video Webcast.

6. What should a Web developer consider when shooting original video for a Web site?

7. List the steps in capturing, editing, and saving a digital video for the Web.

8. List some things to consider about the audience for your Web site, as you plan for including video.

☆ Hands-On Exercises

1. Find three examples of uses of video on a Web site: one that entertains, one that explains a process, and one that tells a story.

2. For each of the videos you found in Exercise 1, identify whether it is streaming or downloaded, and determine its file format and pixel size.

3. Develop a storyboard for a short video you might use on a Web site. Include visual, audio, transition, and timing information.

4. Based on the storyboard you developed in Exercise 3, shoot some original video footage, capture and edit it with video-editing software, add titles and transitions, and save it in a form suitable for a Web site.

5. Embed or link the video you prepared in Exercise 4 into a Web page.

CHAPTER SIX

INTERACTIVE MEDIA ON THE WEB

This chapter looks at two forms of interactive media on the Web: virtual reality (VR) and interactive elements. You'll explore examples of the possibilities offered by each medium, and you'll learn how they work on the Web. You'll learn how to create a simple VR panorama, how to develop interactive elements, and how to include these forms of media on your site. Along the way, you'll learn about some of the software tools that are used to develop interactive media.

Chapter Objectives

- To understand the potential of virtual reality on the Web
- To find out how VR panoramas and objects work
- To understand how to create a simple VR panorama using common software and hardware tools

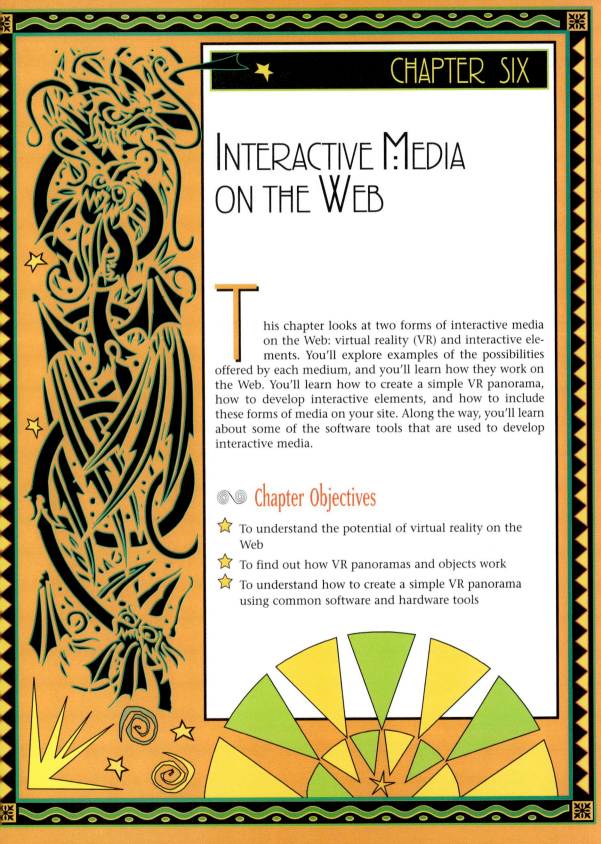

☆ To learn how to embed a VR panorama or object into a Web page

☆ To understand the potential uses of interactivity on the Web

☆ To know how interactivity works on the Web

☆ To understand the process of creating a simple interactive element using Macromedia Director or Flash

☆ To learn how to embed an interactive element in a Web page

◎◎ The Possibilities of Virtual Reality on the Web

It's a pretentious name: **virtual reality**. What poses as virtual reality on the Web is seldom close to physical reality. It's really a form of multimedia with aspects of images, animation, and video along with interactive user control. Most VR on the Web is in the form of **VR panoramas**—scenes in which you feel as if you're moving around or inside a room or other location—and **VR objects**, which you can rotate and manipulate in space as if they were in your hand.

Also found on the Web are VR "worlds" created with **Virtual Reality Modeling Language (VRML)**. These three-dimensional environments contain textured geometric shapes created with 3-D **computer aided design** (CAD) and modeling software and then exported in VRML. This is not a common format on standard Web sites, and few computers have the needed plug-ins. Moreover, the tools for developing these VR scenes aren't commonly available. So we focus on the more common and accessible panoramas and objects. For more information on VRML, see the Online References section.

VR Panoramas

On the site of WGBH (`http://broadband.wgbh.org/qtv/`), visit *This Old House* to tour the Charlestown house interior before and after its transformation (see Figure 6.1). Look up, down, and around the staircase. Zoom in to see how the details of the new bathroom sink reflect the building's historical architectural details. Or sit inside the New Beetle at the Volkswagen Web site (`http://www.vw.com/newbeetle/360cam-2.htm`), and twist your head around (using your mouse) to see what's left, right, ahead, and behind you. Focus on the speedometer. Notice that there are three cup holders up front, but only two seats. Take a virtual walk around the lobby of the Renaissance Hotel in Massachusetts (`http://RenaissanceHotels.com/dpp/PropertyPage. asp?MarshaCode=BOSSB`), and then work your way through the luxurious standard room. At your own pace.

These VR panoramas look like normal pictures on a Web page until you click and drag the mouse inside them to reveal that you're "inside" a scene and can look around as you wish by moving the mouse. They're **interactive** panoramas because users determine where and how to look around.

Figure 6.1 Typical Web Site VR Panorama

These kinds of panoramas are made by positioning a camera on a tripod in a fixed place and taking a series of pictures in a 360-degree circle. Then these still images are stitched together with special software into a single continuous scene and are saved in a format that can be read with a VR player plug-in.

When you encounter a panorama on a Web page, you see only a single view of the scene. As you click and drag the mouse, the VR player plug-in presents you with other parts of the scene in a continuous scroll. Many panoramas let you look up and down as well as left and right, using the same technique.

VR Objects

Examine the Nissan Pathfinder in your virtual hand, looking at it from left, right, front, and rear, at the car manufacturer's Web site (`http://www.nissancanada.com/eng/cars/pathfinder/360exterior.html`). Click the mouse to open the hood and look at the engine. Or visit the gallery of Goldsmiths 3 (`http://www.goldsmiths3.com/gallery.html`), and hold a ring, rotating it and zooming in to see the details of the gold work and the shimmering jewels. Ever been to Fort Yellowstone? If you can't go there, visit the Web site of the National Park Service (`http://www.nps.gov/yell/tours/vr/ftyell3a.htm`) and hold in your hand an historic padlock from the early days of the fort, looking at it from all sides.

These experiences are based on **VR objects**, special files that contain views of an object from many angles. In response to mouse movements, the VR plug-in moves these objects smoothly to give users the impression of holding the object in their hand. Dozens of separate photographs of the object, taken at various angles, are stitched together using the VR development software and saved in a format that permits their realistic display through the VR plug-in.

These VR techniques permit users to perceive and understand the scene or object in ways that are impossible with still images, video, or animation. Because they are under user control and because they mimic the natural ways in which we interact with the world, VR panoramas and objects can be effective communicators on a Web site. The fact that many automobile, real estate, hotel, museum, and educational sites employ such panoramas and objects proves their utility.

☆ **DO IT YOURSELF**   **Consider VR**

Find examples of VR panoramas and objects on the Web. Think about where a VR panorama or object might fit on your Web site. What function would it serve for users?

How VR Works on the Web

Just as still images, animations, sounds, and videos on the Web have their own special file formats and are interpreted by a codec in the browser or by a special plug-in, so, too, do VR panoramas and objects. The biggest difference is that VR has no history or tradition from the years before computers were invented; it is a child of the information age. You can't do VR in a magazine or on a TV screen or with a sound system. VR is a totally new form of communication made possible by the computer and well suited to the Web.

VR files are not large—the largest of the samples mentioned here is just over half a megabyte—so they do not suffer as much as sound and video from the bandwidth bottleneck. VR allows for high-quality images and high levels of interactivity. VR panoramas and objects are only a little more difficult to create than original sound or video files. And the plug-ins necessary for a user to experience VR are becoming widely installed. So we can expect a continuing growth of this medium on the Web.

Moving and Zooming

The key distinguishing feature of VR is viewers' ability to change their point of perspective—to look all around in a panorama or to rotate an object. All the popular Web VR systems and examples provide this feature.

A simple VR example lets you move across the screen in a single plane, as if your eyes or the object were remaining on the same level. More complex examples extend this movement up and down, letting you look high on a wall or down at a floor, or letting you see the bottom and top of an object as well as the sides.

Some VR examples also let you zoom in and out, peering more closely at a small part of the scene as if you were walking toward it, or zooming out as if you were stepping back to get a larger view (see Figure 6.2). The more types of movement and zooming that are possible, the more realistic the experience.

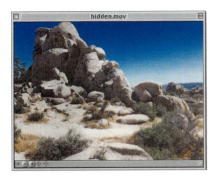

Figure 6.2 Zooming In on a VR Panorama

Hot Spots and Links

Just as you can click on a hot spot in an image map to link to another Web page, you can click on a location in a VR panorama or object to link to something else. You might link to another panorama, as in the Renaissance Hotel example described earlier. Or you might link to an illustration, as in the Nissan example. By linking with these hot spots, the Web developer can create a complex tour of a building or city, letting users move from panorama to panorama. Click on a door, and move into the kitchen, another panorama (see Figure 6.3). Click on another door to enter the bathroom, and so on. These links add to the interactivity of the experience, making it seem more "real."

Figure 6.3 Linked Panoramas on a Web Site

File Formats and Compression

Each VR system uses its own file format, which can be read only by its player. Most of what's stored in this file is the data from the continuous image that was created from the separate photos. The rest of the data in the file provides information on the nature of the file, the lens angle at which the pictures were taken, and the compression algorithms that were used. The VR player uses this information to display the panorama or object correctly.

Because the data in these files is mostly images, the JPEG compression algorithm is most commonly used, just as it is employed in compressing still images. The various techniques of image compression described in Chapter Two can be applied to VR files, something that explains their small size.

VR Players

The plug-in that displays a VR image takes part of the image data from the file and places it in the window so that it looks natural. To do this, the player distorts the image slightly, making it somewhat rounded (see Figure 6.4). Then as you rotate left or right with the mouse, the image seems to flow as if your eye and your head were rotating. You're not aware of this distortion. If it's done correctly, your view of the scene or object seems to flow naturally.

Figure 6.4 Flat Stored Image (Left) and Distorted Displayed Image

◎◎ Creating VR for the Web

To create VR for the Web, you need a camera, a subject, a rotating device, and VR creation software. You shoot the pictures, use the VR software to stitch them together, and save the file in the proper format.

Hardware Tools

You can use any kind of camera, but one with high-quality optics and high resolution will produce better results. Professional VR developers often use 35mm film cameras or high-resolution digital cameras, but you can get adequate results with a point-and-shoot film or digital camera. It's handier to use a digital camera because the images are already in digital form and you don't have to send out the film for processing and digitizing.

Cameras that can take a 360-degree view automatically, using special mirrors and lenses or mechanical rotators, are also available but not in common use.

To shoot a VR panorama, you need a device that can hold the camera steady as you rotate around the circle to take the shots. A tripod is essential for this purpose. One that's fitted with a special device marked off in degrees makes it easier to space the shots evenly.

⭐**TIP**   In a pinch, you can use a DV camcorder to create VR because most of them have a still image mode. But the low resolution of these images, and the extra steps necessary to get them from the camera and convert them to a still image format, make the camcorder a second choice.

To shoot a VR object, you need something that can hold the object steady as you rotate it through the 360-degree circle. For simple work, this can be a turntable. The camera stays in one spot as the turntable is rotated.

Software Tools

VR panorama and object creation software takes the series of images from the camera and **stitches** them together into a single picture. It also provides tools for adjusting and editing the images, and it helps you save the file in one of the common Web formats. An example is VR Worx from VR Toolbox, Inc. Other software that can help you cretae a panorama include Apple QuickTime VR Authoring Studio, iPix Immersive Imaging, and Photovista from MGI.

Development Techniques

To develop a VR panorama, follow the steps described next. (To create a VR object, you follow similar steps. The main difference lies in how you take the pictures.)

Setting Up the Equipment

⭐**WARNING** When you take the series of still images, shut off the flash. Using flash will introduce inconsistencies in the lighting of the images.

Locate the best viewing point for your panorama. It's usually in the center of the area, but it might also work well from a point just inside a doorway, especially if you plan to link rooms in your project.

⭐**TIP**   Use a carpenter's level to level your tripod. The bubble level on some tripods is not accurate enough.

Set up the tripod on solid ground, and make sure it's perfectly level. It's important that the camera be level so that the images match exactly as you move around the circle. If you have one, place the turning device on the tripod. Then mount the camera.

Taking the Pictures

For a simple panorama, using a standard lens, you should take at least 12 pictures. (A more detailed panorama would call for a narrower lens and more pictures.) If you have one, set the turning device to the number of degrees between each picture. (Divide 360 degrees by the number of photos you plan to take. For example, 12 photos means 30 degrees; 16 photos works out to 22.5 degrees.) If you have no turning device, make your best estimate.

⭐**WARNING** Photo Inconsistency

Because the panorama will include photos taken at different times, changes that occur as you take the picture can cause anomalies. For example, a cloud can suddenly appear and block the sun, changing the brightness and color of part of the scene. A person can appear in one photo near the edge, but not in the overlapping adjacent photo, and foul the stitching. Take the pictures as quickly as you can, and be on the lookout for changes.

Look through the viewfinder as you take each picture to make sure it overlaps with the one before it and that there are no anomalies in the photo. The software will use these overlaps to do its stitching. Don't budge the tripod as you move around.

Importing the Images into the VR Software

If you use a digital camera, the images are most likely in JPEG format and ready to import into the software. As you import the images into the software, it will query you about the focal length and lens angle of your camera as well as the number and pixel size of the photos. When the settings are correct, the VR creation software loads the series of images into its memory.

> ★ **SHORTCUT**   If you use a film camera, you will need to develop the film and then digitize the images. The PhotoCD process accomplishes both steps with a single trip to the camera store.

Editing the Images

Most VR creation software lets you edit your images, rotating them to the correct orientation, adjusting brightness, removing anomalies, and so on. Usually, little editing is necessary, but it's a good idea to look at each image. Now is the time to repair any anomalies or add things that weren't there in real life.

Stitching the Images Together

Now is when the software pays for itself. It does the stitching automatically, matching the edges of one picture with the next. The software compares the adjacent images pixel-by-pixel, looking for similarities and then aligning them exactly. Some editors let you set the tolerance for this matching, which may need to be adjusted for photos that are blurry or contain lots of similar vertical elements close together. When the stitching is finished, the software displays the tapestry for you in a long horizontal scroll, as shown in Figure 6.5.

Figure 6.5 A Stitched Panorama

Blending the Stitched Images

Because the photos were taken at different times, at different angles to the light, and with a tripod that may not have been exactly level, the left edge of one image will not be exactly the same as the right edge of its adjacent image. You can see these mismatches in Figure 6.5. So at this step, the VR creation software blends these edges, correcting differences in color and brightness, moving pixels to match the edges of objects, even blurring areas where an exact match is impossible. You can often set the desired extent of blending and blurring at this point.

Creating Hot Spots

If you plan to link your panorama with another scene or with another Web page or resource, now is the time to create the hot spot. You define the spot using a rectangle or other shape, and then you choose the VR file or enter the URL of the Web resource that you want to link to (see Figure 6.6). A scene can contain multiple hot spots.

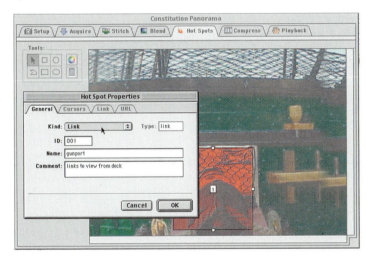

Figure 6.6 Adding a Hot Spot with VR Worx

Compressing the Data

You now have a wide panoramic image, stitched and blended, perhaps with a few linked hot spots. The software will compress the data in this file, in most cases using the JPEG algorithm, and may allow you to set the amount of compression to apply. The sample panorama shown in the illustrations compressed to 628K.

Exporting the File

The software writes the file to the disk in the format you choose. As you do this, you also choose the part of the scene where the user will enter the panorama along with other factors affecting the display.

The most popular format for VR panoramas on the Web is the QuickTime VR file format, which is viewable with the standard QuickTime plug-in. The file is saved in the appropriate media directory on the Web server.

☆ **DO IT YOURSELF**   **Create a VR Panorama**

Follow the steps outlined here to create your own VR panorama or object.

◎◎ Embedding VR in a Web Page

Like sounds and images, VR panoramas and objects can be embedded in a Web page so that they appear integrated with the text and images on the page. Or they can be launched from a link and open in a separate window. If you like, you can also display a controller with buttons for zooming and finding hot spots.

Embedding VR with a WYSIWYG Web Page Editor

Embedding a VR file using an editor such as Dreamweaver is very similar to inserting a video or a sound. Follow these steps:

1. Place the pointer at the location where you want the VR to appear.

2. In the Insert menu, click Media, and then click Plug-in.

3. In the file section dialog box, choose the VR file from the proper directory, or type its URL. A square with a plug-in icon appears in the document window at the pointer location. This square represents the VR.

4. Stretch the square to the length and height of the VR, such as 320 pixels wide and 240 pixels high. If you plan to show the controller bar at the bottom, add another 16 pixels to the height of this square.

5. Preview the page in the browser. (The default setting for embedded VR is to show the controller.)

You will see the VR with its controller, and the VR will be ready for use as soon as the page and the file are loaded.

Embedding VR with HTML

To embed a VR file with HTML, use this code:

```
<embed src="/media/vrpano.mov" width="320"
height="256"></embed>
```

The name of the VR file here is `vrpano.mov`, and it's in the media directory. The panorama will show 320 pixels wide and 256 pixels high with its controller.

Linking VR with a WYSIWYG Editor

You can use a linked VR when you want your audience to see the panorama or object in a new window. You can also use one to let your audience click a button or word to bring up the VR file. When the link is clicked, the VR opens in its own window. To link a VR from a Web page, follow these steps:

1. Select the item you wish to link from. It can be a word or phrase in the text, a button, an image, or a hot spot in an image map.

2. Click Make Link from the Modify menu.

3. Click the folder icon. In the file selection dialog box, navigate to the VR file, or type its URL.

4. Click OK, and the link is made.

5. Test the link by previewing the page in a Web browser.

The nature of the window that displays the VR will depend on the plug-in that's used to play it. QuickTime uses a plain window with a simple controller bar.

Linking VR with HTML

To link to a VR from a Web page using HTML, use this code:

```
Here is the <a href="/media/vrpano.mov">link</a>.
```

In this example, `link` makes a link to the VR file `vrpano.mov` in the `media` directory.

> ☆ **SHORTCUT**   This is the same code that's used to link to any other URL on the Web.

Whether your VR is linked or embedded, you may need to add text to tell viewers that this is indeed an interactive VR and not just a still image (which is what it looks like when it appears). And if you have not included a controller, you may have to tell them how to move around and zoom in and out.

☆ **DO IT YOURSELF**   **Link VR**

Use a WYSIWYG editor or HTML code to link to a VR from a Web page. Test it in both browsers.

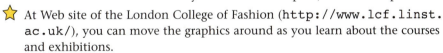

◎◎ The Possibilities of Interactivity on the Web

If you want to explore the possibilities of using interactivity on the Web, here are a few examples:

 At the Timex Web site (`http://www.timex.com/interactive/icontrolRINGSET.html`), you can operate the ringset of the new iControl watch. You move the ring to the stopwatch position and start the timer. Then you listen and watch as it counts down. To see how many seconds have elapsed, click the Stop button.

☆ At Web site of the London College of Fashion (`http://www.lcf.linst.ac.uk/`), you can move the graphics around as you learn about the courses and exhibitions.

☆ On the Biology Place Web site (`http://www.biology.com`), you can conduct a classic experiment on the effects of various wavelengths of light on the growth of a plant. You can also construct a hydrocarbon molecule by dragging its elemental atoms into place (see Figure 6.7).

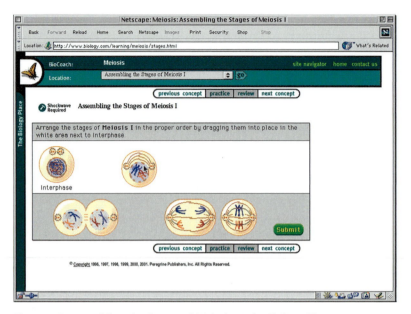

Figure 6.7 Assembling the Stages of Meiosis at the Biology Place

★ Need a refreshing sweet treat? Visit the Ricola interactive Herb Garden (`http://www.ricola.com/herbgarden/garten.htm`) and explore the science and art of flavoring through a combination of panoramas and interactive quizzes.

★ If you visit the MTV Web site (`http://www.mtv.com/nav/intro_busta.html`), you can play the online game *Busta Sensei*, and face the bad guys at the Tunnel Club with various kicks and escape moves.

These interactive sites—some game-like, others manipulatory—are designed to get users involved directly with the subject. Not only do users control these experiences, but also the sites respond to users. When you turn the ring on the watch, for example, it actually moves and clicks. The endless possibilities of this form of communication are only beginning to be exploited on the Web.

These examples, like many others, were built with Macromedia Director and Flash and can be played by the Shockwave-Flash plug-in. The key feature of such interactive experiences is that users manipulate objects with the mouse and see (or hear) the direct result of their actions.

Interactive experiences on the Web are used to

★ Entertain, such as when you play a fast-paced game, to keep your attention so that you'll look at the advertisements

★ Educate, such as when you manipulate the variables in an experiment and then conduct it to see the results

⭐ Market products, such as when you operate a watch or an automobile on the Web page and it responds as it would in real life

DO IT YOURSELF   Consider Interactivity

How might interactivity help communicate essential ideas on your Web site? What would be the nature of the interactivity?

◉ How Interactivity Works on the Web

Like most other multimedia, interactive elements for the Web are developed with special software, saved in a particular file format, and played via a plug-in installed on users' browsers. The plug-in and the development software are made by the same manufacturer and work closely together. Interactive software and plug-ins are constantly being improved, so the possibilities for growth in this kind of media are endless. They aren't restricted by the limitations of HTML and the standard browsers.

With these systems, you build a small computer program using a general-purpose development environment such as Macromedia Director, a general-purpose programming language such as Java, or a specialized development tool such as Flash. Usually, this program is self-contained and could run even without a Web browser. For this reason, you can build almost any kind of interactivity or media into the program. When this program is embedded in a Web page, the browser is simply acting as a conduit for it; the browser doesn't interpret the code in the program. Instead, the code is interpreted by the plug-in (Shockwave, Flash, or Java) that displays and operates the program.

These development environments provide interactive capabilities that are not possible with HTML, including the following:

⭐ *Manipulation of objects*. Users can drag items with the mouse and drop them into place, as in the Biology Place example.

⭐ *Animation*. Text and objects can move in a variety of ways controlled by the developer or the user, as in the *Busta Sensei* example.

⭐ *Immediate response to user actions*. The user's actions can trigger an immediate response, as in the Timex watch example.

⭐ *Entry of data by the user*. The user can type numbers or text from the keyboard or make choices with the mouse. The program can remember and respond to this input with logical results.

⭐ *Immediate calculation of and response to user input*. The user can type a loan amount, term, and interest rate, for instance, and the program can calculate internally—without recourse to a server or database—a monthly payment.

★ *Logical analysis.* From simple if...then analysis to complex logical combinations, the program can consider a variety of factors—including time, date, history, and user responses—and deliver a unique, customized result.

★ *Integration and coordination of multiple media types.* Sound, video, text, images, and animation can be coordinated—with each other and with the user's actions—to produce immediate multimedia interactivity.

Creating Interactivity for the Web

This brief guide cannot provide a complete course in Flash or Director programming. Many books are available for those purposes. Instead, this chapter introduces these three popular tools for creating Web interactivity and explains briefly the process of using them.

Macromedia Flash

Of the three tools, Flash is the easiest to learn and use. Its chief strength lies in creating animation, as explained in Chapter Three, but Flash can also be used to build interactive elements. You can program objects to respond to user actions, and you can perform simple logic using variable expressions and **action scripts**, which are logical subroutines carried out in response to an event on the screen. Figure 6.8 shows the process of building a simple script.

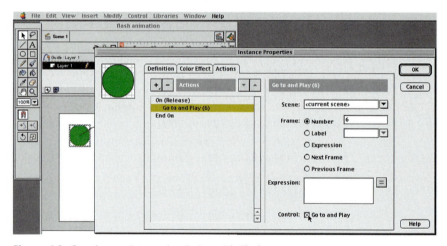

Figure 6.8 Creating an Interactive Script with Flash

  Flash can handle graphics, sound, and animation, coordinating them well. Flash files using vector graphics and compressed sound are small and efficient, traveling over the Web swiftly and requiring the widely installed Flash plug-in for playback.

Macromedia Director

Director is the granddaddy of Flash. Director is a bit harder to learn and more extensible in terms of potential interactivity. You can use it to import and interact with almost any form of media, including video, sound, images, text, Flash animations, databases, and Web resources. Its Lingo scripting language is a rich and extensible programming environment that has few limitations in implementing interaction. The newest version has added three-dimensional objects and spaces to its repertoire. Director files are played by the Shockwave plug-in. Figure 6.9 shows how a simple logical script is developed in Director.

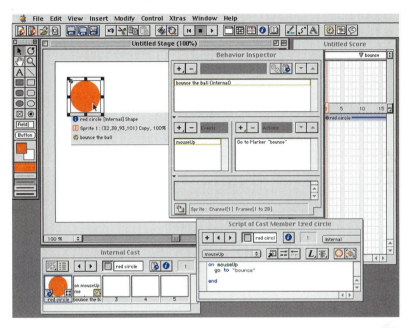

Figure 6.9 Building an Interactive Script with Director

The Online References section lists Web sites that have more information about each of these software tools. Other tools, too, are available. Some Web sites include interactivity based on Java applets, CGI scripts, server-side database functions, Visual Basic, Web Objects, QuickTime, and others. And new tools and techniques are being invented as this book is written.

Development Techniques

No matter which tool you use to develop an interactive element for the Web, the development process is similar. It follows these steps:

1. Determine the purpose, scope, and sequence of the interactivity. Typically, you produce a written document that describes what will happen, why, how it will be developed, and how it will be delivered to users.

2. Draw a flow chart. This will be a more complex diagram than the simple linear flow chart you created for your video in Chapter Five. It will include logical branching ("if the user drags the ball into the basket, increment the score by 2 points") as well as program flow and choices.

3. Prepare the media elements. Typically, you develop the images, sound, music, backgrounds, video, and text outside the programming environment and save them in the proper format.

4. Import the elements. With Director and Flash, you import (or create) each media element as you would with other high-level programs: by clicking Import from the File menu. In Director, the elements are stored in the **cast**; in Flash, they reside in a **library**.

5. Bring the elements into play. In Director, you drag the media elements from the **cast** onto the **stage**. In Flash, they go from the **library** onto the **stage** (see Figure 6.10). Flash also provides a **timeline** along which the action proceeds; in Director it's called the **score**.

> ☆ **SHORTCUT**   Director and Flash provide special tools for developing vector graphics from scratch, something that can make the process more efficient.

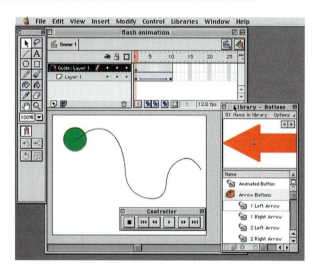

Figure 6.10   Timeline and Stage in Flash

6. Program the logic and interaction. In Director, you do this by assigning **behaviors** to various cast members, such as "if the user clicks on the ball, play the bouncing sound and move the ball six pixels to the right." In Flash, these are called **actions**.

7. Test the interaction. Run the **movie**, as it's called in both Director and Flash, and see whether it works. Revise as necessary, and test again.

8. Export the file. When everything works according to spec, export the file in a compressed format that can be played by the standard plug-in. With Flash, create an `.swf` file, and with Director a Shockwave `.dcr` file. The files reside in a directory on the Web server.

9. Test with various browsers and platforms. Embed the interactive file in your Web page, and test it under Explorer and Netscape and on Macintosh and Windows.

10. Revise the file based on the results of the test, and publish it on the Web server.

◎◎ Embedding Interactivity in a Web Page

Like other media that require a plug-in, interactive elements are most often included in a Web page using the EMBED tag. The method of including an interactive file in Flash (.swf) or Shockwave (.dcr) format is similar to that for embedding sound or video.

Using Web Page Editors

Dreamweaver makes it easy to embed Flash and Shockwave files. Follow these steps:

1. Make sure your Flash or Shockwave file is in the right format (.swf or .dcr), that it's saved in the proper directory on the Web server, and that it has a Web-legal filename.

2. From Dreamweaver's Insert menu, click Media, and then click either Flash or Shockwave, as shown in Figure 6.11. Dreamweaver will in most cases automatically set the width and height of the embedded object and set it to play automatically and to loop.

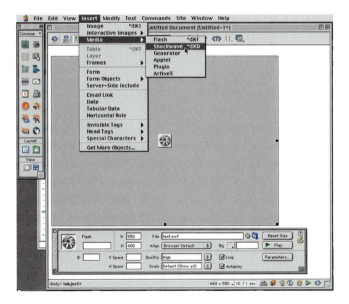

Figure 6.11 Embedding an Interactive Element with Dreamweaver

3. Try out the interactivity by clicking the Play button in the Properties window, as shown in Figure 6.11.

4. Test the Web page with interactivity by clicking Preview in Browser from the File menu.

Other Web page editors may not provide the automatic sizing and play parameters that Dreamweaver does. You may need to embed these kinds of files in the same way that you embed sounds and videos, adding the width, size, and display attributes yourself.

Using HTML Tags

The EMBED tag is used to include Flash and Shockwave files:

```
<embed src="test.swf" pluginspage="http://www.
macromedia.com/shockwave/download/" width="550"
height="400"> </embed>
```

★**TIP**   For a Shockwave file, the extension would be `.dcr` instead of `.swf`.

Plug-ins and User Experience

These kinds of interactive elements will not play on your visitors' computers unless they have installed the latest plug-in. To help visitors, be sure to include a pointer to the Web page where they can download the necessary Shockwave or Flash Player plug-in. This pointer is added automatically by Dreamweaver but not by other Web page editors. It's also a good idea to include text, such as "Requires the Flash player," with a hypertext link to the download page.

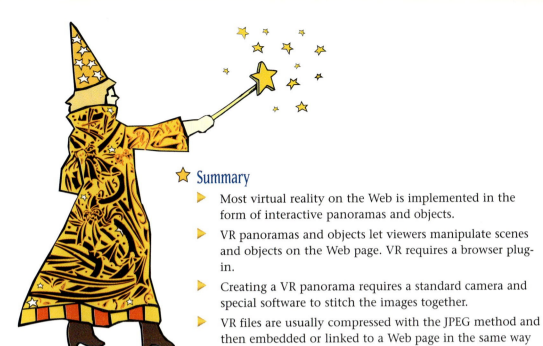

★ Summary

▷ Most virtual reality on the Web is implemented in the form of interactive panoramas and objects.

▷ VR panoramas and objects let viewers manipulate scenes and objects on the Web page. VR requires a browser plug-in.

▷ Creating a VR panorama requires a standard camera and special software to stitch the images together.

▷ VR files are usually compressed with the JPEG method and then embedded or linked to a Web page in the same way as sound or video.

▷ Interactivity on the Web is used to entertain, educate, and market products.

▷ Interactive elements allow user manipulation of objects and various responses to user actions, as well as other forms of multimedia and interactivity.

▷ Flash and Director are often used to create interactive elements for the Web, which are displayed with the Flash Player and Shockwave plug-ins.

▷ Interactive elements are most often embedded in a Web page in a manner similar to sound and video files.

★ Online References

Panoguide, a reference for tools and techniques for creating VR panoramas
http://www.panoguide.com/software/fileformats.html

A reference site for QuickTime VR authoring
http://www.apple.com/quicktime/qtvr/

Sites for other VR panorama software tools
http://www.mgisoft.com/products/webtools/panorama/
http://www.ipix.com/products/immersive_stills.shtml

Frequently asked questions about VRML
http://home.hiwaay.net/~crispen/vrmlworks/faq/faq1.html#q1

Online sample files and tutorials on using Flash
http://www.macromedia.com/software/flash/productinfo/tutorials/

Online tutorials and references for using Director
http://www.macromedia.com/support/director/

☆ Review Questions

1. List three reasons to use a virtual reality panorama or object on a Web site.

2. Explain at least two key features of VR panoramas or objects on the Web.

3. List the steps in creating a VR panorama for the Web.

4. Describe some of the things that must be considered when shooting photographs for a VR panorama.

5. How might an interactive element be used to accomplish the objectives of a Web site?

6. Describe the software tools and processes used to create simple interactive elements for the Web.

7. Explain how scripts are used in Flash and Director to develop interactivity.

☆ Hands-On Exercises

1. Find on the Web at least three interactive panoramas or objects. For each, define its purpose on the site, and determine which system was used to produce it.

2. Following the instructions in this chapter, create a VR panorama or object movie.

3. Embed or link the VR that you created in Exercise 2 to a Web page.

4. Use Flash or Director to create a simple interactive element for a Web site.

5. Embed the interactive file you created in Exercise 4 into a Web page, and test it in both browsers.

APPENDIX: ANSWERS TO ODD-NUMBERED REVIEW QUESTIONS

◎◎ Chapter One

1. Multimedia on the Web can be viewed at any time, not just during the scheduled broadcast. Multimedia on the Web is, for the most part, smaller in size and lower in quality than the same media on television, radio, or magazines. Multimedia on the Web is more often presented in combination with text and cross-references. The viewer generally has more control over the selection, starting, and stopping of the media on the Web.

3. The bandwidth bottleneck can prevent some viewers from receiving multimedia information in a timely fashion. Sound and video are especially demanding of bandwidth, and the Web developer must take into consideration the bandwidth enjoyed by a typical user of the site, as plans are made for multimedia.

5. A codec—compressor/decompressor—applies mathematical algorithms to the data in a computer file so that the size of the file is reduced as much as possible, but the information in the file is degraded as little as possible. Codecs use the techniques of removing repetition, averaging, range reduction, selectivity, and frame difference to compress multimedia files.

7. The nature of the multimedia viewing experience will vary depending on the speed of the viewer's processor, the nature of the video circuitry and display, the viewer's knowledge of and willingness to install plug-ins, the type of operating system, the type and settings of the viewer's Web browser, the nature of the local network and firewalls, and the computer hardware platform. These can affect the speed, quality, and accessibility of multimedia for the viewer, especially sound and video files.

◎◎ Chapter Two

1. Images on a Web site can provide facts, explain a process, set a mood, evoke an idea, pinpoint a location, or illustrate a relationship. An image can be a photograph, a sketch, a painting, a symbol, a logo, a diagram or a graph.

3. GIF works best with simple images of plain lines and areas of solid color. JPEG works best with photographs, and images with complex and gradient colors. The two compressors use very different algorithms, designed specifically to work with the two different types of images.

5. Photographs on film or on paper, drawings, pictures taken with a digital camera, still images from videotape, items from a scanner—all provide sources for images. Images can also come from other Web sites, or from CD-ROM collections. A scanner is necessary if the image is on paper or on a slide, to convert the image to a digital computer file. Digital cameras and drawing programs provide files that are already in digital form, and need not be converted. The same is true for images from the Web or from CD-ROM.

7. Expanding the display size of an image simply enlarges each pixel, causing the image to become blurry and indistinct. The image will not appear satisfactorily to the viewer. If you need to display an image larger than life size on a Web page, you should scan or prepare it at a higher resolution.

◎◎ Chapter Three

1. Animation can capture the viewer's attention, animation can entertain, it can explain a system or process, and it can set a mood.

3. First, you must prepare each of the individual images that make up the animation, usually in a drawing or image-editing program. Then you must import these frames into an animation-editing program. Here you test the animation, making sure it operates correctly. As you save the animation, you compress and optimize it, in the GIF format, and place it in the proper directory on the Web server.

5. Animations can be created with Adobe Photoshop's Image Ready, with macromedia Fireworks, with Macromedia Flash, with GIF Builder, or GIF Animator.

7. Animations prepared with Flash or Shockwave can be more complex, contain interactivity, incorporate sound, and work well in smaller file sizes. But some users may not have the necessary plug-in, or enough memory to run the animation and its plug-in adequately. Also, the act of finding and installing a plug-in is difficult and confusing for many users.

◎◎ Chapter Four

1. On a Web site, sound can convey information, set a mood, capture attention, explain a process, or provide a sense of personal contact. Music, sound effects, and the human voice can be used separately or in combination to achieve these purposes. But the Web developer must be careful when using sound. Unsolicited sound can disturb and disrupt the viewer. Sound requires a plug-in

that some users may not have. And sound requires much more bandwidth than text or images, making it difficult for modem-users to enjoy.

3. To work in a computer, sound must be digitized, converted from its natural analog form to a digital form. The pitch and volume of each split second of sound is recorded as a number. The frequency of these recordings is called the sampling rate of the sound. The file of numbers is saved in a file on the computer disk in one of the many sound file formats. When the file is opened, the computer converts the digital representation of the sound into a continuous analog signal that is played through the speakers or headphones.

5. Downloaded sound transfers an entire sound file from the Web server to the user's computer. The sound does not begin to play until the file has completed its download. Streaming sound downloads and plays second by second, as it arrives from the Web server to the user's computer. A downloaded sound remains on the user's hard drive, while a streaming sound does not.

7. The sound must first be captured, and then digitized by sound editing software. Then the digital file is modified, in most cases using the same software. Often several sources of sound are combined in multiple tracks. When complete, the sound file is compressed saved in a format suitable for the audience of the Web site. The file is placed on a Web server. Finally, the sound is embedded or linked in a Web page.

◎◎ Chapter Five

1. Video can tell a story, entertain an audience, explain a process, or bring a personal touch to a Web page. Video can bring sound, movement, and dynamism to an otherwise static site. But video demands substantial bandwidth, which may be beyond the capabilities of many Web viewers. And all video needs a plug-in to display in a browser. The many competing plug ins for video can make its reception over the Web difficult for some users.

3. Video compression codecs use the techniques of eliminating repetition, tokenizing patterns, averaging, range reduction, and frame difference to reduce the size of a video file. Repeated data and patterns of data in the file are identified, and recorded as a token to save space. Light and color information is averaged in ways that are not very perceptible to the human eye. The dynamic range of this information is also reduced so that it can be represented with a number of lower precision. And, as much as possible, the codec records not every pixel in every frame, but only those that change from frame to frame.

5. A live streaming video Webcast needs a video camera and a microphone to capture visual and audio information. This information is transmitted over a wire to an encoding computer, which digitizes the audio and video, and packetizes it so it can be sent over the Internet. These IP packets are received and distributed by a streaming video server to various members of the audience.

7. First, the equipment must be connected — the source of video to the computer. Then the video information must flow to the computer, where it is digitized (if its source is analog) and saved to a file on the computer's hard disk. The video is combined with other information (still pictures, narration, music, other video clips, and titles) with video editing software. When complete, the video is compressed and saved in a format suitable for the audience of the Web site. The compressed file is placed on the Web server, where it is linked to or embedded in a Web page.

◎◎ Chapter Six

1. VR can let the viewer experience a place in ways that are impossible to achieve with text, images, or video. Whether panorama or object, the viewer can interact with the scene or the item by manipulating it directly on the screen. The Web publisher can provide an experience through VR that helps the viewer understand the reality, work his way through it, or be led to purchase it.

3. First, a series of still pictures are taken in a 360-degree circle. If not already in digital form, the pictures are converted to individual image files on the computer's hard disk. These images are brought into panorama-creation software that stitches the pictures together into a single continuous image. The image is then saved in one of the VR file formats suitable to the Web. Its is compressed and saved to a Web server. From here the VR is linked or embedded in a Web page.

5. Interactivity can be used on a Web site to gather information from users, to get users involved directly with the subject or products of a Web site, to entertain users so that they stay with the site or the product, and to educate them through simulations and other devices.

7. Scripts allow the interactive element to respond to user actions in a variety of ways, including linking to another interaction or Web page, testing to see if a condition is met in the element, scoring user actions, moving objects on the screen, and performing calculations.

INDEX

CREDITS

Figures 1.1, 1.8, 2.2, 2.9, 2.14, 2.15, 3.4, 3.5, 4.1, 5.1, 6.1	Screen shot(s) reprinted by permission from Microsoft Corporation.
Figures 1.3, 1.9a, 1.9b, 2.1, 3.2, 3.3, 5.2, 6.7	Netscape Communicator browser window © 1999 Netscape Communications Corporation. Used with permission. Netscape Communications has not authorized, sponsored, endorsed, or approved this publication and is not responsible for its content.
Figure 1.8	Courtesy of Weather.com © 2001, The Weather Channel Enterprises, Inc. All rights reserved.
Figures 1.9a, 1.9b	Web pages reproduced by permission from Dorling Kindersley Ltd.
Figure 2.1	Courtesy of Dr. Mark A. Lawrence (www.monalisaprofile.com)
Figures 2.4, 2.7, 2.10, 2.12, 2.13, 3.8, 5.15	Adobe, PhotoShop, and Premiere are either registered trademarks of Adobe Systems Incorporated in the United States and/or other countries.
Figures 3.3, 6.7	© 1986–2001 Peregrine Publishers (http://www.biology.com)
Figures 3.9, 3.13, 4.10, 4.11, 5.10, 5.11, 5.12, 5.14, 5.16, 5.17	Screen shots reprinted by permission from Apple Computer, Inc.
Figure 3.14	Cinema 4D XL by MAXON Computer (www.maxon.net)
Figure 6.1	© 2000, Volkswagen of America, Inc.
Figures 6.4a, 6.4b, 6.5, 6.6	Interface © 2001, VR Toolbox, Inc.